Mindful Co-working

Be Confident, Happy
and Productive in Your
Working Relationships

Clark Baim

D0145210

Jessica Kingsley *Publishers*
London and Philadelphia

First published in 2014
by Jessica Kingsley Publishers
73 Collier Street
London N1 9BE, UK
and
400 Market Street, Suite 400
Philadelphia, PA 19106, USA

www.jkp.com

Copyright © Clark Baim 2014

Front cover image source: iStockphoto®. The cover image is for
illustrative purposes only, and any person featuring is a model.

All rights reserved. No part of this publication may be reproduced in any material
form (including photocopying of any pages other than those marked with a ✓,
storing it in any medium by electronic means and whether or not transiently
or incidentally to some other use of this publication) without the written
permission of the copyright owner except in accordance with the provisions of
the Copyright, Designs and Patents Act 1988 or under the terms of a licence
issued by the Copyright Licensing Agency Ltd, Saffron House, 6–10 Kirby Street,
London EC1N 8TS. Applications for the copyright owner's written permission
to reproduce any part of this publication should be addressed to the publisher.
Warning: The doing of an unauthorised act in relation to a copyright work
may result in both a civil claim for damages and criminal prosecution.

Library of Congress Cataloging in Publication Data
Baim, Clark.
  Mindful co-working : the art of working together with
confidence and enjoyment / Clark Baim.
       pages cm
  Includes bibliographical references and index.
  ISBN 978-1-84905-413-3
  1. Teams in the workplace. 2. Interpersonal relations.
3. Interpersonal communication. 4. Work
environment--Social aspects. I. Title.
  HD66.B32 2014
  650.1'3--dc23
                                    2013036952

British Library Cataloguing in Publication Data
A CIP catalogue record for this book is available from the British Library

ISBN 978 1 84905 413 3
eISBN 978 0 85700 803 9

Printed and bound in Great Britain by Bell & Bain Ltd, Glasgow

Contents

Acknowledgements

I am grateful for the collaboration and ideas of many colleagues who have helped me develop as a co-worker and to think through the concepts in this book. I am profoundly grateful, first and foremost, to Mary Leyland, with whom I co-worked for nine intense years between 2000 and 2009. During our time as co-workers and co-trainers, working internationally, together we generated and refined many of the concepts in this book. We also trained several thousand professionals in the practical skills of mindful co-working. Mary has recently retired, and in my mind she remains the quintessence of the mindful co-worker. She models like no other the simple act of caring. She has devoted herself to protecting children, working with troubled families, helping people make life-saving changes, and training professionals to do the same. It was a pleasure and a privilege to co-work with her during what will always seem to me to be a golden period of work in my life, with the added bonus that this was work with a very dear friend.

I am also indebted to other people with whom I have had the privilege of co-working. On reflection, I seem to have been rather prolific in seeking opportunities to co-work. My best work has always come from collaboration with others, and recognizing this I wish to thank my co-workers past and present, including Lydia Guthrie, Susie Taylor, Fiona Macbeth, Tony Morrison, David Middleton, Joanna Bell, John Richards, Jane Wiffin, Joe Sullivan, Richard Bradbury, Dawn Fisher, Kerry Malone, Anita McLeod, Elizabeth Hayes, Richard Swann, Mel Thornton, Kristina Hofberg, Bridget Rothwell, Trudi Annetts, Jinnie Jefferies, Manuela Maciel, Jorge Burmeister, Alun Mountford, Sally Brookes, Andy Watson, Louise Heywood, Despina Visantiadou, Sanja Jagaric, Vedran Korusic, Annei Soanes, Peter Haworth, Sheila Foxgold, Bron Roberts, Peter Holden, Mark Farmer, Toni Philippides, Liz Murphy, Jackie Canicle, Panna Modi, Di Willetts, Roger Kennington, Gail McGregor, Dan Wilcox, Rita Donathy, Rosie Bampton, David

Cook, Jenny King, Yvonne Rose, Gail Reed, Pat Lloyd, Clive Davies, Sally Tarpey, Jenny Stead, Keith Garrison, Sue Hunt, Sue Dunford, Ted Eames, Lynne Strong, Denise Hill, Dreda Wisniewska, Janet Cockerham, David Snooks, Ryan Hamilton, Emma Smallman, Mark Robinson, Mark Farrall, Hilary Dawson, Juliet Raynsford, Victoria Lee, Andy Marshall, Jez Thomas, Ken Guy, Ian Pringle, Jon Watson, Steve Morris, Dominic Somers, Tom Mellor, Yvonne Gregory, Kerry Reidy, Irene Brown, Adrian Dakers, Rhiannon Sawyer, Sue Deedigan, Jackie Evans, Karen Sweeney, Mark Londesborough, Camilla Gibbs, Saul Hewish, Simon Ruding, Patrick Tidmarsh, John Bergman, Tom Swift, Dan Brown, Ian MacKinnon, Shaun Landry, Scott Stevens, Mike Bael, Jill Reinier, Katy Emck, Ken Walker, Una Morton, Shannon Smy, Jim Tysver, Jo Hathaway, Jan Alcoe, and colleagues at Cheswold Park Hospital. I am very lucky to have met and collaborated with such dedicated and creative colleagues, and I am grateful for what I have learned from each of them about the art and craft of co-working. I also acknowledge and thank the many national and regional trainers, facilitators, customers and clients who have offered many suggestions for refinements along the way.

During the draft stages, a number of people have offered valued insights, feedback and suggestions for which I am very grateful. These include Chris and Joanna Brown, Clive Leyland, Lydia Guthrie, Liz White, Jeanne Burger, Patricia Crittenden, Sue Daniel, Annette Jackson, Pam Miranda, Sandie de Wolf, Amanda Kevin-Tidis, Marg Hamley, Amanda Jones, Trish McCluskey and many other colleagues at Berry Street/Take Two, Anna Mason, Christine Boal, Eden Baim and Alyson Coupe. I am also very grateful to the ever-encouraging team at Jessica Kingsley Publishers, including Steve Jones and Sarah Hull, and the cover designer Yvonne Booth.

Introduction

TWO OPENING VIGNETTES

As I was writing this introduction, two news headlines caught my eye. The first item read, 'Doctor loses a tooth in operating theatre bust-up.' Two senior hospital doctors in Manchester, England – one a consultant surgeon and the other a consultant anaesthetist – reportedly fought each other in the hospital corridor over what began as a disagreement about the right process for bringing patients to the operating theatre on time. During the altercation, one of the doctors lost a tooth.[1]

The second item, covering events on a far larger scale, was headed, 'Military sex abuse rattles capital'. The story was prompted by US Defense Department research estimating that 12,100 of the 203,000 women and 13,900 of the 1.2 million men in the US armed services experienced a sexual assault from fellow military personnel in 2012. This was 7000 more assaults than the previous year. President Obama and lawmakers on Capitol Hill were sharply focused on the issue, expressing zero tolerance for sexual harassment in the military.[2]

Such sobering tales of violence and abuse in the workplace are certainly not unique; similar problems of interpersonal conflict and sexual harassment are found in many workforces, not just the medical field and the armed services. This violence and abuse, occurring

---

1 *Daily Telegraph* (2013). 'Doctor loses a tooth in operating theatre bust-up.' Available at www.telegraph.co.uk/news/newstopics/howaboutthat/10009885/Doctor-loses-a-tooth-in-operating-theatre-bust-up.html, accessed 2 May 2013.

2 Steinhauer, J. (2013, May 9) 'Military sex abuse rattles capital.' *New York Times Global Edition*, p.7.

in the working environment and among colleagues, may be seen as extreme forms of co-working gone wrong. It is behaviour that is strongly influenced by the environment and the organizational culture, and as such it can be foreseen and to a very great extent prevented. And while violence and sexual abuse in the workplace are shocking and awful, it is important to place them in the context of known behaviours, behaviours that we understand, and behaviours that are at the extreme end of a continuum of negative behaviours in the workplace that include at one end lack of interest or disharmony, worsening towards suspicion and hostility, and at the extreme opposite end, acts of violence and abuse. Wherever these behaviours are on the continuum, they can be predicted and largely curtailed with the right approach.

Thinking about solutions in the context of this book, it strikes me that the two doctors and the armed services chain of command might gain something from a more considered approach to respectful co-working and collaborative colleagueship. Developing the craft of mindful co-working and collaboration would to a very great degree prevent such conflicts in the future and lead to improved performance and effectiveness in hospitals, in the military and in any workforce where employees work in close proximity with each other or where cooperation and collaboration are important parts of the job.

THE IMPETUS FOR WRITING THIS BOOK

The stories of the two doctors and abuse in the military are typical of a common problem in the modern workplace: the lack of attention given to developing the principles and skills of mindful, respectful co-working. The stories also demonstrate that problems with co-working can arise at all professional levels; status and seniority do not automatically bestow a good attitude towards co-working or co-working skills, and rivalry and fractious relations can exist among lower ranking employees right up to the top echelons of the organization.

During 25 years of working together with many colleagues in a wide range of corporate, public sector and non-profit settings, I have seen close-up how important it is to get the principles and skills of co-working right. As a trainer, psychotherapist, workshop leader and team supervisor, I have observed hundreds of co-working relationships, and have seen the ingredients that make for happy and effective co-working in pairs, teams and organizations. In most situations where co-working has gone wrong, it is because one or more of the workers – perhaps the entire organization – have assumed that good co-working should 'just happen' if you bring competent people together. Sometimes, this does happen, but very often it doesn't. This book is designed to optimize the chances that co-working is effective, collaborative, non-discriminatory and enjoyable for all concerned – and highly beneficial to the overall aims of the organization or company you work for.

I have also had the great pleasure of passing along some of these insights to other people during more than 2000 training workshops and in numerous conferences, team development, supervision, coaching and consultancy commissions in 15 countries. Many participants and colleagues have offered new ideas based on their experiences of 'going live' with the method. This feedback has helped to refine what I and my colleagues call *mindful co-working* – a method that makes co-working both more enjoyable and markedly more effective and sustainable over the long term.

DEFINING CO-WORKING AND WHERE IT IS USED

Co-working is where two or more colleagues collaborate to deliver their work or accomplish a task or common goal. This includes professional training and development, group work, social care, media and communications, business and industry, education, criminal justice and policing, sports, aviation, the health and legal professions and many more settings and contexts. Indeed, the principles and skills of mindful co-working apply to any occupation or organization where working together with others is a part of the job.

WHAT IS *MINDFUL CO-WORKING?*

The term 'mindful co-working' reflects a simple truth: the best co-working happens when colleagues pay purposeful and careful attention to their own and each others' roles, responsibilities, thoughts, feelings and perspectives. It requires a conscious and deliberate use of the mind and the imagination. In other words, mindful co-working does not happen by chance, or by rote delivery. It is always a result of fully conscious and considered collaboration.

The use of the word 'mindful' is also related to the increasingly popular use of mindfulness meditation,[3] which in turn has deep connections not only with ancient Buddhist practices but also with modern developments in interpersonal neurobiology.[4] This book does not have space to give a full recounting of mindfulness and interpersonal neurobiology, so it will suffice to say here that truly mindful co-working is deeply dependent on how each person manages their own thoughts and feelings, and this in turn has a profound effect on the people they interact with. Multiply this effect across a significant portion of the workforce, and you will have a transformed working environment. Indeed, in recent years a growing number of small and large companies have woken up to the powerful effects of integrating mindfulness practices into the working day.[5] Mindful co-working is in some ways an extension of this idea, but it does not rely on meditation. The key is that mindful co-working is fully conscious and purposeful co-working, as opposed to being routine or unfocused.

Many people have reported that they find mindful co-working to be professionally liberating because it removes the tension and pressure of one-upmanship from the co-working relationship, replacing these negative forces with a spirit of openness, mutual support, equality and creative collaboration. They have reported benefits that include better communication and respect among colleagues, improved morale, consistency of performance, better team cohesion and ultimately, improved results for the clients, service users, customers or patients – and therefore the organization or business as a whole. This translates into better performance and

3   Kabat-Zinn, J. (2005) *Full Catastrophe Living: How to Cope with Stress, Pain and Illness Using Mindfulness Meditation.* New York: Bantam Dell.

4   Siegel, D. (2007) *The Mindful Brain: Reflection and Attunement in the Cultivation of Wellbeing.* New York: Norton.

5   Tugend, A. (2013, March 22) 'In mindfulness, a method to sharpen focus and open minds.' *New York Times.* Available at www.nytimes.com/2013/03/23/your-money/mindfulness-requires-practice-and-purpose.html?_r=1&, accessed 12 October 2013.

improved results in all types of organization, however success is measured. Mindful co-working contributes to a virtuous circle of communication in the workplace, where thoughtful and respectful interaction among colleagues leads to more of the same, at all levels of the organization. For any agency, organization or company, it pays to invest in the development of mindful co-working skills.

By contrast, many professionals I have spoken with have reported a range of previous negative experiences when co-working has gone wrong. They recall instances when poor co-working has led to antagonism, gossip, insecurity, resentment, jealousy, bullying and formal grievances among colleagues. This creates a toxic atmosphere in the organization that works against its aims and mission. Poor co-working also tends to lead to professionals working in isolation, even when they work alongside colleagues, and ignoring or de-valuing – and sometimes taking credit for – each others' contributions. Poor co-working can lead to highly regressive and infantile behaviour being acted out in the workplace – not to mention worker burn-out, high staff turnover, work overload, impoverished staff development and poor organizational performance.

This book offers an antidote: a practical, accessible guide to the skills of mindful co-working. Having experienced its benefits, I want to pass on what I have learned about co-working to people in a wide range of settings, because the principles and skills of mindful co-working apply everywhere people work together.

VARIATIONS OF THE WORD 'CO-WORKING' IN DIFFERENT CONTEXTS

In this book, the term 'co-worker' is used to stand for many different types of co-working, joint working and team situations. However, if you use different terminology, that's fine. For the term co-workers, you can substitute:

- *colleagues*
- *team members*
- *staff members*
- *associates*
- *crew*
- *co-facilitators*

- *co-trainers*
- *co-presenters*
- *co-tutors*
- *co-teachers*
- *co-leaders*
- *co-therapists*

- *co-pilots*
- *co-drivers*
- *co-captains*
- *co-authors*
- *co-directors*
- *co-creators*
- *team mates*
- *squad/platoon members*

- *committee/panel members*
- *party members*
- *partners*
- *band-mates*
- *family members (however you define family)*
- *members of the tribe*
- *or any other term you use.*

Even though different terms may be used, wherever colleagues work together to co-deliver any type of work, the principles and skills of mindful co-working will apply.

Similarly, the terms *customer, client, participant, patient, audience* and variations of these terms are used in the book. Again, if you use different terms to speak about the beneficiaries or end users of your service or product, please substitute the terms that fit best.

THE POWERFUL EFFECTS OF MINDFUL CO-WORKING

Here's what people notice when they observe mindful co-working in action:

- They notice colleagues who work in true partnership and who communicate with respect, care and attention to each other.

- They see colleagues who are collaborative, alive to each others' ideas and input: colleagues who show that they value each other, and who bounce around ideas and get energy from each other with good humour.

- They observe anti-discriminatory and non-oppressive practice in every aspect of the co-workers' interaction with each other. They notice colleagues who genuinely appreciate each other and who show authentic interest in each others' perspective, knowledge and feelings.

- They notice professionals who treat each other as equal human beings and who are willing to share power in decision-making, even when one has far greater seniority, status, authority or experience.

- They see co-workers who appear to work seamlessly together and in mindful anticipation of each others' contributions. They seamlessly pass the baton back and forth, and when they are really tuned into each other, it can look as if they are reading each others' minds. There is no sense of workers showing off or trying to steal the limelight. Instead, the work is shared at a deep level.

- They see colleagues who call on each others' expertise and who delight in each others' strengths. Similarly, they see colleagues who help each other to shore up any weaknesses, and lend support when needed.

- They observe colleagues who seem more relaxed, because they do not carry the whole burden of responsibility on their shoulders. They see workers who feel confident in each others' presence and who share responsibility at a meaningful level.

- They notice the trust that exists between the co-workers, which also leads to transparency and open and clear communication between the workers. They notice that there are no hidden agendas between the workers that detract from the focus of the work or session.

- They notice colleagues who share the same ethos and the same goal in relation to the work they are undertaking or the content being discussed. There is no hint of colleagues working against each other.

- They experience colleagues who can motivate people. There is an inspiring 'can do' atmosphere which is infectious, creative and productive. This helps to create a safe environment where people will be encouraged, supported and affirmed.

- They notice, if a man and a woman are co-working, how a man and a woman can collaborate without any hidden agendas, self-doubt or regression to gender stereotypes.

They see a respect for difference as well as an endorsement of equality.

- They notice, if two women or two men are co-working, how work can be shared between them without competition or collusion with gender stereotypes, whatever they may be. They observe co-workers who feel secure enough with each other to carry out their work effectively and also to ask for assistance.

The feedback from thousands of people who have adopted this approach to co-working has been highly consistent: they say, simply, that it works. The benefits are often immediate and powerful. Colleagues who are working together for the first time, and also colleagues who have been working together for years, find that in applying the skills and principles of mindful co-working, their work becomes more effective and productive – and remarkably less stressful.

MINDFUL CO-WORKING AFFECTS THE 'BOTTOM LINE'

Whether you work in the corporate world, industry, the public or charity sectors, or anywhere else, great working will have a huge impact on the 'bottom line' of worker performance and organizational effectiveness. Across the entire working spectrum, co-working is a crucial factor in job satisfaction and effectiveness at work. A 2002 study funded by the European Union found that almost 100 per cent of respondents said that co-working and communication skills are an important part of their job.[6]

The emerging field of workforce science, which relies heavily on numbers-crunching from terabytes of data from thousands of organizations across the world, has shown some remarkable

---

6   Oskarsdottir, G., Busetta, P., Ginestie, J. and Papoutsakis, H. (2002) *Employability Skills in Non-Professional Occupations: A Four-country Comparative Research Project.* Reykjavik: University Press, University of Iceland.
       This study compared a range of employment issues in four European countries. Among numerous findings, co-working skills and communication skills were seen as important in all job categories in all of the countries researched. Almost 100 per cent of interviewees in all countries said that cooperation with co-workers was a very or somewhat important skill.

and unexpected results about what makes the difference in staff effectiveness and staff retention. For example, recent research has shown that the quality of supervision is probably more important than the individual attributes of the worker in determining the effectiveness of the worker's contribution. Research of employees' current performance compared with their prior track record with other firms is showing that the past is not always a good predictor of future results. Where there is good quality supervision, this is now understood to be a crucial factor in determining an employee's tenure and performance – even more crucial than their employment history.[7] It seems reasonable to hypothesize that mindful co-working would enhance this effect even further. Empirical research will be needed to test this hypothesis.

The findings from the 'big data' research certainly match the impressions I have gained from speaking with colleagues about co-working. Most people I have spoken with about co-working have said that their most satisfying experiences at work – aside from their interactions with clients, customers or patients – have been their co-working relationships and what they gained through collaborative working. It's often a major reason why people stay with an organization and do good work – because of the quality of their relationships and their resulting commitment to their colleagues and the organization.

Here are some of the benefits to the organization when co-working goes right:

- improved services for customers, clients, patients or participants, that is, a better product or service[8]
- better staff retention
- improved knowledge retention and innovation
- improved integration of distributed leadership processes
- improved efficiency in training new staff

---

7   Lohr, S. (2013, April 21) 'Scientific management redux: the difference is in the data'. *New York Times*. Available at http://bits.blogs.nytimes.com/2013/04/21/scientific-management-redux-the-difference-is-in-the-data, accessed 12 October 2013.

8   See, for example, Atul Gawande's 2009 book, *The Checklist Manifesto* (London: Profile Books), for important findings regarding dramatic improvements in surgical outcomes when surgical teams pause to check in with each other at three points: before anaesthesia, before incision and before leaving the operating theatre.

- continuity of standards of service
- better communication and respect among colleagues
- improved morale among staff
- more satisfying working relationships
- the positive 'ripple effects' among other staff and staff groups, and among customers or clients, when they witness and experience the beneficial effects of positive co-working
- if your work is with high-risk populations and in multi-disciplinary settings, there will be improved public protection and safeguarding, because there are more 'eyes' and perspectives on the situation, and the people involved feel better able to communicate with and trust each other.

CO-WORKING IS EVERYWHERE

Once you start to think about co-working and what it really means, you start to notice it everywhere. We all instinctively know what good co-working looks and feels like, and we have plenty of examples in popular culture and all around us. Think Fred Astaire and Ginger Rogers, or watch any well-functioning sports team, or even a busy, happy and well-run restaurant, and that's a start. Or you could watch any 'buddy movie' or think about myriad stories, novels, films or television dramas where the central character needs other people to help them face a challenge or go on a journey, mission or quest. All of these stories – often summed up as the popular story telling tradition of 'the hero's journey'[9] – capture a deep truth about the human condition: that we are not alone, that we need each other, and that one of our primary purposes in life is to help each other get through this journey together – whatever form that help takes. All of this reminds us that we are often better together; great co-working partnerships are more than the sum of their parts, and arise from our basic instincts as a social species.

---

9   Campbell, J. (2008) (First published 1949) *The Hero with a Thousand Faces*. Novato, CA: New World Library.

A CAVEAT – AND A BONUS

A key message of this book is that great co-working does not 'just happen'. It comes as a result of conscious and deliberate communication between colleagues, across a range of topics and practices, and over time. Hence, a word of caution: the most solid and lasting co-working relationships can only develop over time.

But there is an implied bonus to this: while learning and developing good co-working relationships can take time, the skills and practices of mindful co-working, once developed, are largely transferable to other co-working situations. What this means in organizations is that, once everyone in the organization learns the principles and skills of mindful co-working, they can shift, exchange roles and re-form into different working arrangements, still using in the newly formed groups the principles and skills they have previously practised. When everyone is signed up to the same co-working principles, collaboration happens more quickly and more efficiently, and organizations thrive.

HOW TO USE THIS BOOK

This book is meant to be a practical guide. It offers general principles, practical skills and also some worksheets for you to copy or adapt and use in your everyday working practice.

This handbook can be used by pairs or teams of co-workers, by supervisors, by trainers and also by whole organizations.

GUIDE TO THE CHAPTERS

Chapters 1 to 6 cover the key principles and working practices of mindful co-working.

Chapter 7 looks at things that can go wrong, and how to remedy them.

Appendix I covers some of the principal features of mindful communication between colleagues.

Appendix II offers some scenarios for discussion and training.

Chapter 1: The five principles of mindful co-working

This chapter captures the essence of mindful co-working by explaining the five principles that apply to virtually all co-working situations. The principles are not meant as firm or didactic rules that must be followed, but instead as points of guidance for you to discuss, adapt and apply with your colleagues, finding the best fit for your context and organization.

Chapter 2: The ten key skills of mindful co-working

Mindful co-working means that you know not only the aims and desired outcome of any work you are undertaking, but also the structure of the co-working you will follow as you collaborate on the work. This chapter builds on the principles and skills from Chapter 1 and describes the specific procedures for optimal co-working. The skills apply to most co-working situations, and particularly in situations where you are making joint presentations or leading groups or activities with a co-worker. Chapter 2 explains in detail the two main types of co-working typically used in these situations, and the techniques and 'rules of the road' that can be used to achieve the most integrated and productive co-working.

Chapter 3: Establishing common ground between co-workers: getting it right from the start

Before colleagues deliver work together, they will benefit from taking time to establish common ground with each other. This means that the workers strive consciously and deliberately to build mutual trust and develop a greater understanding of each others' strengths and areas under development. When workers establish this common ground, they also develop a deeper appreciation of each other as human beings, and a better understanding of each others' attitudes, beliefs and working practices in relation to the aims of the organization. Chapter 3 offers a series of topics for co-workers to discuss in order to establish common ground and working practices.

Chapter 4: Planning together

Mindful co-working requires deliberate planning – not only of the content of the work to be done, but also of the process that workers will use and who will be responsible for what. Planning sessions are also valuable opportunities to anticipate how to help each other to develop professional skills and confidence. Chapter 4 provides guidance about how to structure planning sessions so that they enhance the effectiveness of your work, and also contribute to your professional development.

Chapter 5: De-briefing

After delivering work together, it is important for colleagues to take time to de-brief. This usually involves discussion about how well they met their intended aims, how they worked together, their thoughts and feelings about the work undertaken, and any notes for future development and follow-up. Giving and receiving constructive feedback is a crucial part of this process, and this should be handled sensitively and respectfully. Chapter 5 offers guidance about how to structure de-brief sessions, and also some suggested ideas for giving and receiving feedback.

Chapter 6: Supervision for co-workers

Most organizations and businesses will have structures in place to offer regular supervision, line management, mentoring or coaching support to staff. These forms of support vary widely in their format and structure, and can offer benefits such as managerial oversight, staff support and development, and, where needed, mediation among colleagues and teams. Where colleagues jointly deliver work, supervision, line management, mentoring or coaching sessions are an opportunity to reflect on and improve co-working practice. Co-workers often benefit from undertaking this support work together. Chapter 6 offers ideas about how supervision, line management, mentoring or coaching can enhance the effectiveness of co-working. It also suggests several practical suggestions for structuring supervision.

Chapter 7: Ouch! Pitfalls to avoid and handy hints when things go wrong

Even with the best of intentions, co-working can still go wrong in little moments and also on a larger scale. When this happens, it can be useful to be prepared in advance for such eventualities. Chapter 7 offers a range of advice and tips for how to deal with fractures in the co-working relationship.

Appendix I: Features of mindful communication between adults

Appendix I focuses on a range of important features of mindful communication between adults generally, and also in the workplace. It uses findings from a range of theories and models in order to offer a summary of what it means to be psychologically 'well' and what it sounds like when we relate to others in a balanced, mature and adult manner. This is crucial information, because mature communication is at the heart of mindful co-working.

Appendix II: Scenarios for discussion and training

In Appendix II, a range of co-working scenarios are described, with the intention of prompting discussion and debate. Key questions for discussion include: What do you think is happening in the interaction, both on the surface and underneath? What could be done to help the co-workers to identify and repair the difficulty they are experiencing? How can similar situations be forestalled? It hands the topic of co-working fully over to you and your colleagues.

CHAPTER 1

The Five Principles of Mindful Co-working

In this chapter, you will learn:

- a rating scale that will help you and your colleagues reflect on the level of functioning of your current co-working
- the five principles of mindful co-working – applicable to pairs, groups, teams, departments and whole organizations.

Chapters 1 and 2 are meant to be read and considered together. Chapter 1 explains the five general principles applicable to all or most co-working situations. Chapter 2 extends these principles and explains the ten key skills of co-working. Together, the two chapters cover the principles and skills that can help you achieve mindful co-working.

ASSESSING YOUR CO-WORKING – FOR PAIRS, TEAMS, DEPARTMENTS AND ORGANIZATIONS

Let's start by doing a quick diagnostic rating of your own co-working situation or your team, group, department or organization. Have a look at Table 1.1. Where are you on this continuum in relation to your own co-working? Where are other pairs and teams in your organization? If you work in multiple teams, as many people do, you can rate the various teams you are a part of. Are you familiar with any other pairs, teams or organizations that function particularly well? What do they do that you could learn from?

Don't worry about precisely which point on the scale a rating should be. Some teams or organizations may function at several places on the continuum, and this can change day to day. The idea is to gain a broadly accurate picture of current functioning. You can use the three columns on the right to assess where you were a year ago (if that's relevant), where you are now, and where you'd like to be in one year (or any other time frame that fits). By setting a goal for the future, you can stay solution-focused and develop an action plan to get there. You can use the ideas and structures in this book to help you get there.

1. Where are you on this continuum in relation to your own co-working?

2. Where are other pairs and teams in your organization?

3. How about your organization as a whole?

4. What changes do you think would help? How can you and your colleagues work together to make those improvements?

5. Are you familiar with any other pairs, teams or organizations that function particularly well? What do they do that you could learn from?

6. How can you use the principles, skills and processes in this book to help you get to where you'd like to be as a team or organization? What is your role in such a transformation?

TABLE 1.1: RATING SCALE FOR CO-WORKING

No.	Level of functioning Pair, team, group, department or organization being rated (e.g. 'My team' or 'My organization'):	One year ago	Now	One year from now (goal)
1	**Mindful co-working** – where people work consciously to optimize co-working and continuously monitor, repair and refresh their collaborative communication. The system is robust and reflective; ruptures lead to discussion and improvement and the system becomes stronger as a result. This is the spontaneous and creative 'dance' of high-level co-working and is the focus of this book.			
2	**Routine or passable co-working** – this can be effective co-working, but there is nothing inspiring about it. There are missed opportunities for developing or improving skills, and workers do not reflect on their interpersonal processes or improve them. Co-workers follow well-known patterns and repeat them – a bit like the film *Groundhog Day*. This level of co-working is vulnerable to becoming rigid or stuck – see item 3.			
3	**Rigid but respectful co-working** – playing it 'by the book'. This can include long-term co-working situations where patterns have become stale over time and stuck in a rut. Processes may be very inefficient and out of date. Co-workers may be dogmatic about the 'way we do things here'.			
4	**Parallel working** – competent workers, but with little or no collaboration (i.e. many lost opportunities for collaboration). People looking after themselves and their own patch. 'Silo' thinking predominates.			
5	**Unequal co-working** – e.g. some workers doing most of the work, with others doing significantly less. This can cause significant friction and degenerate into resentment and animosity.			

TABLE 1.1: RATING SCALE FOR CO-WORKING *CONTINUED*

6	**Cold shoulder co-working** – workers resisting collaboration or reluctant to cooperate with each other. Group-think predominates, with little or no challenge of the status quo.			
7	**Suspicion and negative competition** – workers wary of each other, watching their backs. Self-protective strategies predominate. Welcome to the rat race. Prepare for back-stabbing and one-upmanship.			
8	**Hostility** – workers actively dismissive about or rude to each other or talking behind each other's backs. This is a highly volatile situation and can quickly lead to staff absence, burn-out, protest and grievance.			
9	**Aggression, harassment and scapegoating** – workers threatening to each other or acting out against individuals in the group. People will be in flight/fright/freeze mode and playing out the roles of persecutor, victim, rescuer or abandoning authority figure (i.e. not intervening when remedial action is needed).			
10	**Violence, menace, persecution, abuse and bullying** – acting out in ways that cause significant physical, emotional or psychological distress or harm. This can include criminal levels of violence, abuse and harassment. Fear and anger permeate the system, and most people will either leave or be caught like hostages and may develop 'Stockholm Syndrome'.[1] In most situations, the system will change only when an explosive event occurs such as a media storm, prosecutions, public embarrassment or shareholder/employee/client/citizen rebellion. It's why the world needs whistle-blowers and investigative journalists.			

---

1   Ochberg, F. (2005, April 8) 'The Ties That Bind Captive to Captor'. *Los Angeles Times*. Available at http://articles.latimes.com/2005/apr/08/opinion/oe-ochberg8, accessed 12 October 2013.

THE FIVE PRINCIPLES OF MINDFUL CO-WORKING

The following five principles apply to all or most co-working situations. The first three principles are mainly focused on attitudes, values, beliefs and principles of interaction – in effect, the general approach we take with our colleagues. The latter two principles focus on co-workers as a working unit, in particular their accountability to the organization as a whole, to their clients or customers, and to each other.

As you read through the principles, if you think it will be useful you can self-rate your own co-working and also that of your team, department or organization. You can also use these principles as topics for discussion and development. If you are a trainer, coach, mentor or supervisor, you can use these principles to encourage the development of your supervisees.

Some of the principles may be more or less relevant to your occupation or work setting. I have tried to explain them for the broadest possible use and to capture most working contexts. Even so, you may need to adjust the principles, disregard some or add your own. You can use these five as a starting place and develop your own set.

FIRST PRINCIPLE: MINDFUL CO-WORKERS TREAT EACH OTHER WITH RESPECT

If there is to be any chance for mindful co-working to develop, colleagues must start from the basic principle of respect. This may seem a painfully obvious principle, yet a lack of basic respect from employers or managers to staff, and between and among workers, is still a common feature in too many working environments.

In mindful co-working, respect must be more than skin deep. It should be genuine, emerging from a felt sense that other people are just as important as we are, whatever their station in life. Otherwise, the concept of respect is trite and superficial, and risks becoming little more than a performance of cheery good will, or even worse, a cynical performance for the benefit of onlookers and superiors who may advance your career. So this first principle is not to be misunderstood as synonymous with knowing how to shake hands and look someone in the eye when you are talking with them. The form of respect being referred to here starts from within – it arises from our basic values and beliefs about ourselves and other people.

Unconditional positive regard

Respect includes the basic respect for any other human being as a person with thoughts, feelings, hopes, struggles, values, family, strengths and vulnerabilities – just like anyone else. When we really take to heart what respect for another person means, we are far less likely to exploit or mistreat them. We may disagree with them, and we may even debate fiercely opposing views, yet even so we can do this while conveying respect for them as fellow human beings.

It may be helpful to draw from researcher and psychotherapist Carl Rogers' idea of *unconditional positive regard* for others.[2] This includes within it the idea that when we interact with other people, we should always start from the stance of basic respect towards another person that recognizes our common humanity, even when there may appear to be major differences between us. When we work with the basic principle of respect, it means we treat other people in the organization as just as important as we are, even when we have higher rank or greater seniority. Rogers' concept is particularly important when conflicts arise, because the concept means that, even in the heat of volatile disagreement, people can still maintain a fundamental respect for other people as human beings – flaws, strengths and all. It's a good alternative to going to war with them, on a small or large scale.

The concept of unconditional positive regard is also based on another important idea – that when people experience warmth, respect and being valued, and when the barriers to positive interaction among colleagues are removed, people will to a very large extent make positive changes and connections themselves.

Respectful leadership and earned authority

If the principle of respect is followed throughout an organization, the boss, the owner or the commander treats the new recruit with

---

2   Rogers, C. (1967) *On Becoming a Person: A Therapist's View of Psychotherapy.* London: Constable.

the same basic respect and decency as they treat their immediate colleagues. Everyone has their important role to play. When leaders and bosses convey this deeply held respect for their employees and subordinates, their own authority has far more legitimacy and impact. Without earned authority, their effectiveness is compromised, their employees will not respect them, and the organization becomes less coherent as a result. This is not a minor issue: in a 2009 study of 3000 adults by Britain's Chartered Management Institute, cited by Sennett, 47 per cent of respondents reported that they had previously left a job because of poor management, and 49 per cent reported that they would be prepared to take a cut in pay in order to work with a better manager.[3]

Respect can take many forms, and it is not the same as being 'nice'. In fact, some leaders and bosses maintain a gruff exterior and even blow off steam, get irate and may shout about something that's gone wrong. It may seem counter-intuitive to think that this might be possible while still maintaining respect for every employee, but here is the crucial distinction: managers who shout and holler in the workplace while also maintaining respectful interactions with their subordinates and colleagues manage this because they do not humiliate or shame any individuals or teams. They shout to convey urgency and get everyone's mind focused on the task. They do not shout to punish, expose, embarrass or otherwise act out their aggression and dominance on individuals or groups within their organization. Leaders who use the tin pot dictator or divide-and-rule approach generally lose their authority or drive staff away from the organization. The staff members who stay will be too frightened to make a mistake, and will go into survival mode. Innovation withers along with employees' spirit. It does not bode well for the long-term survival of the organization.

---

3   Sennett, R. (2012) *Together: Rituals, Pleasures and Policies of Cooperation.* London: Penguin, p.171; see also Chartered Management Institute. *Half of Workers Quite Jobs Due to Bad Management.* Available at: www.managers.org.uk/news/half-workers-quit-jobs-due-bad-management, accessed on 26 September 2013.

Boundaries

Respect also includes respect for boundaries. Most complaints in the workplace arise from violation of boundaries.[4] Boundary violations include:

- sexual or physical boundary violations – including sexual contact, invading personal space or unwanted touch
- disrespectful or bullying behaviour: this can include disrespectful eye gaze, suggestive or intrusive remarks or questions, or inappropriate notes or invitations
- intrusive, persistent or inappropriate communication using social media and other electronic communication
- gossip and breaking confidentiality: making private communication and information (including emails, notes, images and recordings) public
- joking or mocking that is offensive or insensitive
- financial exploitation
- deception
- spreading rumours
- emotional manipulation (e.g. emotional blackmail)
- inappropriate interactions with friends and family members of the other person
- gift giving that is too personal in its intent, and which is not welcomed
- taking, hiding or damaging personal property.

Adult-to-adult communication

Another way of thinking about respect is through psychotherapist Eric Berne's concept of adult-to-adult communication.[5] Berne, the founder of the popular form of therapy known as *transactional analysis*, developed the concept of child, adult and parent type communication. Briefly, the child part of our selves is the uninhibited

---

4   Towergate Insurance. 'How to avoid breach of boundaries.' Available at www. towergateprofessionalrisks.co.uk/tips-and-advice/how-to-avoid.aspx, accessed on 12 October 2013.

5   Berne, E. (1976) *Beyond Games and Scripts*. New York: Grove Press.

part, full of uncensored impulses and passions. The adult part is our mature self, able to balance and reflect on thoughts, feelings, plans and relationships. The parent part is the part of us that has 'internalized' the way our parents treated us. This may take a number of forms from loving encouragement, to high expectations, to pressure to perform, all the way to stern admonition, rigidity, punishment or abuse. It is strongly influenced by our parents' style of parenting and our experience of them as parents.

Berne observed that in many aspects of interaction between adults, problematic communication arose when they moved from adult-adult communication styles (i.e. mature communication) to parent-child, child-child, parent-parent, and so forth. Problems are particularly acute when one or both people experienced critical parenting and use this style of communication when they, in turn, speak from the parent position. This is known as speaking from the 'critical parent' role, and it can be highly corrosive in co-working situations.

A key message from Berne's insight is that in the workplace, if communication is to stay respectful and boundaried, it needs to stay on the level of adult-to-adult, especially when there is conflict, high emotion, or difference in status or seniority – all situations in which adult-to-adult communication can easily slip away if people do not consciously attend to their mode of communication.

Respect can be a matter of life and death

As I write this, people are still being dragged alive from the rubble of a building in Dhaka, Bangladesh, where more than 1100 garment and shop workers died after their poorly built multi-storey factory building collapsed.[6] According to reports, the workers had seen cracks developing in the walls in the days prior to the collapse, but their managers and the business owners had insisted they return to work or be fired. Where in this equation is the basic respect for human beings above profit? The problem is of course not unique to developing nations or to profit-seeking corporations; the pattern is repeated in many countries and has been going on for thousands of

---

6   For several weeks after the collapse on 24 April 2013, the unfolding tragedy was reported ubiquitously in the world's media.

years. In organizations large and small, whatever their purpose, we humans all too easily lose sight of our common humanity. In Dhaka, this had deadly consequences.

Questions to consider:
- How respectful is communication in your workplace?
- How consistent is your respectful communication with colleagues?
- How consistent is the respect shown to you?
- What do you think about Carl Rogers' concept of unconditional positive regard? How easy or difficult is it to follow this principle in your workplace? What is modelled by the organizational leaders?
- What is your understanding of boundaries and respect for boundaries in your workplace and occupation?
- What is your estimate of how often communication is adult-to-adult in your workplace?
- What are some practical ways to maintain adult-to-adult communication in your workplace?

SECOND PRINCIPLE: MINDFUL CO-WORKERS BEHAVE IN ANTI-DISCRIMINATORY AND NON-OPPRESSIVE WAYS WITH EACH OTHER

This principle is related to the first, and adds a conscious and deliberate attempt to recognize, understand and work positively with difference. Again, this seems like an obvious point in the modern workplace, yet still it needs reinforcing and firm establishment as a central principle at the core of mindful co-working, because it can so often be lost when systems are under stress or when organizational processes fall into comfortable routines.

Welcoming difference, challenging prejudice

Anti-discriminatory and non-oppressive practice includes welcoming difference and taking the opportunity to learn about other people. It includes active expressions of good will towards colleagues, and conscious and purposeful attempts to work positively, respectfully and without prejudice with people when there are differences in gender, race, age, cultural background, minority status, physical abilities, appearance, body size or shape, intellectual and mental abilities, sexual orientation, religious practices or spiritual beliefs, social class, nationality or regional background, accent or language (including language fluency), rank or status in the organization, socio-economic background, or relationship status.

Anti-discriminatory and non-oppressive co-working also includes challenging stereotypes and remaining scrupulous in attending to subtle oppression that can be part of the status quo of an organization or a whole society. A common feature of most human societies, historically and to the present day, is that one or more categories of people are de-humanized and turned into scapegoats or folk-devils. It is one of our most destructive propensities as a species, and feeds into an age-old cycle of human oppression, violence, conflict and war. It's one of the reasons we need laws and constitutions, to protect minorities, the weak, the vulnerable and people who differ from the mainstream. It is also why organizations, leaders and co-workers need to remain vigilant against oppression and discrimination creeping into the workplace.

The platinum rule

Most people assume that working in anti-discriminatory ways means simply that we treat others as we would wish to be treated – the so-called Golden Rule, which dates back to Confucius. Yet when people have very different life experiences, values and backgrounds from us, if we simply treat them as we would wish to be treated, we may inadvertently act in insensitive ways. What's 'normal' for us may be strange, confusing, offensive or threatening to the other person. Considering this process in reverse, if we interpret other people's behaviour towards us only through the lens of what feels 'normal' for us, we run the risk of misinterpreting the meaning and intent of their communication.

So when working in anti-discriminatory ways, it pays to follow what has come to be called the 'Platinum Rule'.[7] Wherever we can, we treat others as *they* wish to be treated, which may be different to how we would wish to be treated. That's where curiosity and

---

7   Alessandra, T. and O'Connor, M. (1996) *The Platinum Rule*. New York: Warner.

interest come into the picture, because the platinum rule implies that we learn about each other and try to discover something about our colleagues and their view of the world. And where we don't know or don't understand how to account for these differences and help our colleagues, we can find ways of sensitively learning more. Which is to say: *When in doubt, check it out.*

Role reversal

To work in anti-discriminatory ways at a mindful level requires that we not only treat other people with respect, but also that we express a basic curiosity about other people's lives and experiences. This is the basic curiosity that asks questions such as, 'What might it be like to be you in this situation?', 'What are some of the challenges you have faced in your life?' Or, 'How could I look at this situation from your perspective?' The psychiatrist and philosopher J.L. Moreno, who devised, among other approaches, the methods of psychodrama, sociodrama and role play, also developed the widely used technique of 'role reversal' to help people take the perspective of other people in order to increase understanding and resolve conflicts.[8] In the technique, people are asked to exchange places and speak from the other person's position. It is a truly mind-expanding technique, used very widely in therapy, coaching, training and education. Intriguingly, the technique does not require the other person to be present. It can be done in one-to-one supervision, where you would take the role of the other person and speak from their perspective, without them being present. The aim is to expand your awareness of how the other person might perceive a situation, or perceive you and their relationship to you. Reversing roles can also be done anywhere and on your own, in quiet reflection. It is a basic way of understanding other people and their perspective on the world, including their point of view about us and how our behaviour affects them. This technique works nicely when combined with the platinum rule, above.

---

8   Moreno, J.L. (1946) *Psychodrama, First Volume*. Ambler, PA: Beacon House.

It is everyone's business

Non-oppressive behaviour is, of course, everyone's business. It is also a two-way proposition; discrimination, prejudice and stereotypes can operate in both directions, from majorities to minorities, and vice versa. For example, if you are a front-line worker in an organization, how many management-bashing statements have you heard in the workplace, where managers are talked about in de-humanizing terms? Conversely, if you are a manager, how many times in management meetings have you heard derogatory or sweeping statements made about front-line workers?

It seems to be a tendency of our species that we quickly get into us-and-them, black-and-white, all-or-nothing, in-group and out-group thinking. There are firmly understood evolutionary reasons for this, and they connect with ancient struggles for survival in harsh terrain and among rival human groups. These ancient struggles have their modern-day equivalents. Even so, in the modern workplace, we need to guard against such tribal thinking with scrupulous, ongoing attention and self-critique.

This means it is everyone's responsibility to work in anti-discriminatory and non-oppressive ways. Responsibility is shared up and down the organization, from the leadership team to the front-line workers, whatever their backgrounds.

Questions to consider:

- How well understood is anti-discriminatory and non-oppressive practice in your workplace? Does your workplace have a policy in place, and is it followed?
- How consistent is your anti-discriminatory and non-oppressive interaction and communication with colleagues?
- How consistently is this behaviour shown towards you?
- What is your understanding of the 'platinum rule'?
- How able are you psychologically to reverse roles with your colleagues? How accurate do you think you are when you try to understand their perspective?
- Are changes needed? What would be a first step towards making such changes?

THIRD PRINCIPLE: MINDFUL CO-WORKERS USE EMOTIONALLY AND SOCIALLY INTELLIGENT COMMUNICATION WITH EACH OTHER

In mindful co-working, colleagues use communication that is thoughtful about their own and the other person's perspective and feelings.

In recent decades, we have come to recognize that there are many forms of intelligence. Howard Gardner developed the idea that humans possess multiple intelligences.[9] He offers the view that inter and intrapersonal intelligences are as important as IQ. He identifies nine types of intelligence, although the categories are to some degree arbitrary, and other authors have divided the categories differently. The list below draws largely from Gardner, but is slightly adapted:

Types of intelligence

- *Verbal/linguistic:* Learning through the spoken and written word.
- *Mathematical/logical:* Learning through reasoning and problem solving.
- *Visual/spatial:* The ability to 'see' things in one's mind in planning to create a product or solve a problem. A key intelligence needed by architects, artists, navigators and explorers.
- *Bodily/kinaesthetic:* Learning through interaction with one's environment. Dancers and athletes are strong in this. Also, people who have practical skills, such as craftspeople.
- *Musical/rhythmic:* This includes not only auditory learning, but the identification of patterns through all the senses.
- *Naturalistic:* Learning through classification, categories and hierarchies. Quiz show finalists excel in this form of intelligence, and Charles Darwin was an exemplar.
- *Existential:* Learning by seeing the 'big picture'. This intelligence seeks connections to real world understandings and applications of new learning.

---

9   Gardner, H. (1993) *Multiple Intelligences.* New York: Basic Books.

- *Intrapersonal/emotional:* Learning through feelings, values and attitudes.
- *Interpersonal/social:* Learning through interaction with others.

What is emotional intelligence?

Daniel Goleman, in his widely read books, focuses on the last two forms of intelligence, which he calls emotional and social intelligence.[10] Briefly, emotional intelligence is our ability to feel, recognize, name and reflect on our emotions, and then to act in an integrated, mature manner. Having emotional intelligence means that we treat our emotions as a source of information which is just as important as our thinking.

Goleman's definition of emotional intelligence is the widest ranging and most performance-orientated, encompassing abilities beyond the specific processing of emotions, including being able to:

- motivate myself and understand what drives me
- persist in the face of frustrations
- control my impulses and delay gratification
- regulate my moods/maintain emotional resilience
- trust my intuitions when making decisions
- keep distress from swamping the ability to think
- empathize with other people/be conscientious
- maintain rapport and collaborate with mutual influence
- live with hope.

The two-speed brain and its role in emotional regulation

Goleman makes a very useful reference to the 'two-speed' brain – the fast emotional brain, and the slower, cognitive brain. The fast brain is the midbrain, also known as the limbic system or the emotional brain. This is the part of our brain that can process information in milliseconds and can help us to take immediate action when our life is in danger and when those we care for are in danger. This is often referred to as the part of brain responsible for fight, flight and

---

10 Goleman, D. (1996) *Emotional Intelligence: Why It Can Matter More than IQ.* London: Bloomsbury.

freeze responses. If you step into the street and see a car rushing towards you, you don't have time to think; you dash to safety. That is the flight response, and it happens in a split second. Without it we would not long survive as individuals or as a species. It's also the seat of the core emotions that keep us alive and tell us what is important in our lives – emotions such as joy, surprise, fear, sadness and anger. When we feel burning anger that suddenly rises within us when we experience an insult, this is the limbic brain firing away to fully concentrate our attention and take action. Do we fight? Do we flee? Do we freeze? Or – do we take a few seconds' pause to bring in the slow brain for a second opinion? [11]

The slow brain is the cortex, which is responsible for the higher functions of abstract thinking, language, planning, organising, reflecting, perspective taking and many other processes that make our species unique. The cortex is the uppermost part of the brain, the part that gives the brain its distinct folded and convoluted appearance. It's folded to give it more surface area for the trillions of neuronal connections it contains.

The cortex is the part of the brain that is the most recent to evolve in our species and it is also the part of the brain that is the last to develop in each person. It's still developing well into our twenties, which helps to explain why teenagers often are ruled by their feelings and have trouble with consequential thinking when passions are running high; their higher brain is still not fully developed, to contain and mediate the functions of the mid-brain.

Why is this important in the workplace? Put simply, the limbic system, because it operates in milliseconds, can easily 'hi-jack' the brain and shut down the higher functions that the brain is capable of. Emotional hi-jacks can occur in anyone when the pressure and urgency are great enough, but certainly some people are more prone than others, and for all sorts of reasons. When we experience an emotional hi-jack, our emotions rule, particularly the emotions of fear, anger or sadness. In order to function in a mature manner, these emotions need to be balanced with the cortical functions. Otherwise we run the risk of behaving in damaging ways to our colleagues.

How long does it take for the cortex to catch up with the fast-speed limbic system? In the heat of emotion, we need a minimum of six seconds for the two brains to get in synch (it depends on

---

11   Kahneman, D. (2011) *Thinking, Fast and Slow*. London: Allen Lane.

the situation and the person; six seconds is the usual minimum).[12]
So the message is, when emotions are running high, find strategies
for taking a time out, thinking, reflecting, taking a deep breath, or
anything that buys you time to engage the higher functions and
think things through using both your emotional brain and your
cortex.

In a nutshell: bring your whole brain to work, fast, slow and
everywhere in between.

What is social intelligence?

As for social intelligence, this is the ability to use our emotional
intelligence in our interactions with others. This is also known
as 'people skills'. Using our social intelligence, we can work
collaboratively and with some depth of understanding about the
interdependence of mutual collaboration and the effects of our
behaviour on our colleagues. We understand our own thoughts,
feelings and motivations, and we interact with other people with
the recognition that their thoughts, feelings and motivations are
just as important to them as ours are to us. Social intelligence is the
basis for relationships, friendships, and – in the terms of this book
– mindful co-working (see Figure 1.1).

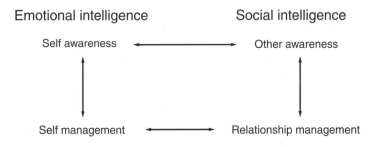

Figure 1.1: Integrating emotional and social intelligence in mindful co-working

Generosity and collegiality

Emotional intelligence also entails a spirit of generosity towards
fellow workers, going beyond mere co-existence actively to promote

---

12   Six Seconds. *Why 'Six Seconds' – About Our Intriguing Name.* Available at: www.6seconds.
     org/2004/02/05/why-six-seconds-about-our-intriguing-name, accessed on 26
     September 2013.

a positive atmosphere among colleagues. This implies a certain degree of friendliness and openness to other people, and an interest in and support of their work, progress and achievements. Another word that captures this spirit includes the word *collegiality,* which might be thought of as courtesy combined with friendly support.

Thoughtful and collegial communication is important for a number of reasons. Perhaps chief among them is that co-working is an 'open-loop' system.[13] This means that the system is interactive and inter-dependent – open rather than closed. Each co-worker is affected by their co-worker(s) and they in their turn have an effect on other people. This includes the effect that co-workers can have on each others' emotions. The mindful approach to co-working therefore needs to take account of people's emotions and their emotional well-being. Here's an example:

> During a joint presentation, your co-worker misses an important detail in a section he is responsible for. Rather than simply correcting him or giving the information yourself, you tactfully intervene by saying, 'George, I recall that in our earlier conversation you mentioned X, and I wondered if you might wish to say something about that?' George looks at you, smiles and warmly thanks you for your prompt. He then covers the missing information and the presentation is improved as a result. During the de-brief afterwards, George thanks you for the prompt, because he recognizes that you are both inter-dependent on one another and you may be feeling like you had intruded on his part of the presentation. He assures you that he welcomes such interventions, and you both feel great about it.

Note that in this intervention, you actually praised George for being a careful planner and endorsed his professional integrity by affirming that he has this knowledge and you know he does. To George, this does not feel like a correction at all, but instead a useful prompt. (George has developed a healthy understanding that co-workers can rely on each other and need each other to do their best work.) To the observers, it will look like an impressive and smooth exchange between two professionals who respect each other.

This is a clear example of emotionally intelligent co-working, because the co-workers are aware of their own processes and requirements while balancing their needs with the needs of their co-worker. These co-workers are tending to the subtle aspects of

---

13   Siegel, D. (2008) *The Neurobiology of We: How Relationships, the Mind and the Brain Interact to Shape Who We Are.* Louisville, CO: Sounds True.

communication that improve rapport and enhance the collaborative spirit. And they are applying the principles in their planning, their presentations and their de-briefing (see later chapters for coverage of these topics).

It is easy to imagine how different the effect would be if you had intervened simply by correcting George or offering the information directly to the audience, without first giving George the opportunity to do this. Can you imagine the thought bubble over George's head if you had done it that way?

The skills of the diplomat – savoir faire and socialité

This form of communication, whether it is between managers and staff or between peers, can have a highly beneficial effect on co-working relationships. Richard Sennett makes the interesting link between this form of communication and the language of the diplomat.[14] Sennett refers to the French concept of *savoir faire*, which is, he points out, more than knowing the right wine to order in a restaurant. *Savoir faire* captures the subtle skill involved in knowing not only how to intervene when needed, but also how to do so in a way that gets the best results for all sides, with particular attention to high emotions and ensuring that no one loses face. Sennett also refers to another French term, not ordinarily used in English: *socialité*. In the French usage, this is the social confidence and assurance you have when you know you can manage conflict and difficulties. It is the manner of the diplomat at the negotiating table, who is open to all sides of a debate, but imperturbable, cool and calm, taking time to reflect before responding. It conveys a mutual awareness and recognition that we are often bound up together in difficult or complex systems and may each have very troubled histories and legacies to contend with.

Here's an example of emotionally intelligent communication that displayed *savoir faire* and *socialité*, that is, the skills of the diplomat, and also the skills of a sophisticated and socially intelligent leader. I observed this exchange at a team meeting of senior managers in a large organization where I was implementing a training programme

---

14   Sennett, R. (2012) *Together: The Rituals, Pleasures and Politics of Cooperation.* London: Penguin.

about emotionally intelligent working practices, so it seems particularly apt that this exchange occurred during the transition process:

The Chief Executive sought to correct a middle manager who was offering what he considered to be out of date and incorrect advice to colleagues in the meeting. This was uncharacteristic of the manager, as she was normally up to date and performing well. Instead of contradicting her or criticizing her in front of her colleagues, he mentioned that he had heard that in a partner organization they were using a new approach that took into account recent changes in legislation. He suggested that 'perhaps we can do some fact-finding together to see if our policy needs updating'. He also endorsed the professionalism of the manager and noted the complexity of the new legislation and how many organizations were struggling to come to terms with new central government guidelines. The manager took the cue and went on to make the correction, redrafting the local policy herself.

When I spoke to her about this some weeks later, she said she was grateful for being allowed to bring herself up to date without losing face in front of her colleagues.

I thought the Chief's intervention was rather sophisticated and empathic towards this manager. Several aspects of his intervention stand out for me:

First, he did not delay in making his intervention. The incorrect guidance was about a serious part of the organization's responsibilities and he could not let the incorrect information be given. The Chief was clearly in touch with the importance of the topic and was able to channel productively what were urgent emotional signals within him. I saw him sit forward and break into the conversation at the earliest opportunity, so it was clear he felt an emotional impulse to speak. He took immediate action yet channelled his emotions into an emotionally and socially intelligent intervention.

Second, the Chief did not thrust himself forward as the authority on the subject or shame the manager for her lack of awareness or incorrect guidance. By referring to the outside agency, he was, with diplomatic grace, deflecting what might have become a head to head debate by metaphorically bringing in outside expertise with a greater authority. Their partner agency, who has a more concentrated focus on this area of the work, had already done the hard work of integrating the new guidelines into practice. The message was that their own organization could benefit from progress made in the partner agency, and needed to get up to speed.

Third, I noticed his use of the word 'we', as in 'we can do some fact-finding together'. He was not leaving this manager out on her own, nor was he making it her sole responsibility to revise the policy. He was letting the manager know that he was present and available to assist, and was giving her support by including himself in the equation. As I understood their working relationship, the manager was unlikely to see this as meddling or intrusion. I think she understood it to be a way of supporting her and not dumping the entire problem at her door.

Fourth, I noticed how he endorsed the manager's professionalism. He referred to a previous version of the policy that the manager had revised, and how useful it had been. He also noted how good she was at forging links with colleague agencies when outside consultancy was called for. This was an important aspect of the intervention, because it affirmed her competence in front of her colleagues.

Finally, I noticed how the Chief Executive normalized the problem when he said that the organization was facing many pressures, including the changes in government priorities and budget cut-backs. By doing this, he was helping the manager and also the whole team to share the load and to recognize how much they needed to pull together to manage the shared burden of their mutual experience. The message to the manager was clear: *the policy needs revision, I am fully confident in your ability to do it, we are all in this together, and you are not alone.*

By the way, my five-part analysis of this exchange, lengthy as it is, should not be taken to imply that the Chief Executive was long-winded; his entire intervention took about 30 seconds. Emotionally and socially intelligent communication certainly does not mean things take longer to say. On the contrary, it is usually a far more efficient way to communicate, and in the long run it means communication becomes more and more efficient as people 'tune in' and build a deeper working rapport and trust. This then becomes integrated as changes are made at the deep and subtle cultural level of the organization. It becomes the way people *are* with each other, and how they think and feel about each other – not just the way they behave towards one another.

Questions to consider:

- To what extent is emotionally intelligent communication used in your group, team, department or organization?
- How often do you consciously try to use emotionally intelligent communication? On what occasions do you slip into less thoughtful communication?
- How generous is the spirit of communication within your organization? How generous are you in your communication?
- What benefits would there be if such approaches to communication were used more often?

FOURTH PRINCIPLE: MINDFUL CO-WORKERS SHARE RESPONSIBILITY AND ACCOUNTABILITY FOR DELIVERY OF THE WORK AND THEIR ROLE IN THE ORGANIZATION

The first three principles of mindful co-working focused on the values and beliefs that underpin mindful co-working, and the manner with which mindful colleagues interact with one another. The fourth and fifth principles focus on our responsibilities towards the organization and to our colleagues.

The fourth principle of mindful co-working is about how colleagues who work together share responsibility and accountability for the quality and delivery of their work. Let's look at some quick examples of co-working situations:

- an architectural team design a new building and see it through to completion
- a surgical team perform an operation
- a team of builders and engineers construct a viaduct
- an ambulance crew rush to the scene of an accident and save lives
- a software company develops and launches a new product
- a team of workers cleans up acres of farmland after a summer music festival
- the teachers and staff of a school collaborate to provide an integrated educational curriculum
- a theatre company rehearses and performs a play

- two co-workers meet to plan and facilitate a group work session
- an airline crew coordinates efforts to carry out a flight
- colleagues in a department store share responsibility for customer service and maintaining the sparkling presentation of the merchandise.

The list is, of course, virtually endless. It is as long as there are types of work involving more than one person. What each example shows is that collaboration – literally, to labour together – is a key to the success of most work settings. Co-working units – whether it be pairs, teams, working groups or tight-knit departments, are at the heart of most organizations and companies. This makes it crucial that colleagues understand their roles in relation to each other and also to the organization as a whole.

Inter-dependence and mutual responsibility

Mindful co-workers recognize that they are dependent on each other for the best results overall for the task at hand and for the organization or project they work for. They work with an understanding that they are responsible together for the outcome. This understanding should permeate every interaction among colleagues, so that tasks are accomplished and information is shared in coordinated ways so that different sub-units and working parties complete their work in synch with other sub-units. Mutual responsibility also means that workers collaborate to find solutions together.

Trust and accountability

Along with mutual responsibility comes mutual accountability. This means that co-workers can rely on each other to do what they say they will do, and to carry out their role and tasks in a predictable and reliable way.

Trust also means that workers can rely on each other to back each other up when work reaches a 'pinch-point', for example when a deadline is looming, when a big order comes through, when a key piece of equipment breaks down and creates a backlog of work, or when a staff member is ill and their role needs to be covered. It also means that co-workers will look out for each other and help each other to make minor or major adjustments as the work goes along.

Team playing

Part of being responsible and accountable to each other is also being a team player. This means sharing responsibilities and tasks, welcoming input from other members of the team, generously sharing ideas, encouraging newer or less confident members of the team, and letting others shine when they deserve it.[15] If you are on the more introverted end of the spectrum, it means finding ways of challenging yourself to interact with other people, to contribute and to get 'in the mix'. If you are on the more extrovert end of the continuum, it means channelling your energies in ways that promote everyone's participation, not just your own.

There is still plenty of room in this approach for star players. But watch the best teams, and where there are star players you will also see coordination and cooperation that ensures the rest of team get a chance to shine, too. We can all think of sports teams where star players have arrogantly dominated the limelight, often with disastrous results for team morale and end of season results. Star players with an attitude of looking out for number one, that is, themselves, can often have a highly corrosive effect on colleagues and erode cooperative behaviour within the team. That might be all right in the short term and gain a quick win, but in the longer term the whole team may be weakened unless a more collaborative spirit is engendered.[16]

Co-working is co-creativity

Great co-working is also an opportunity for creating something new. It might be a new process, a new product, a new programme or simply a fresh way of doing a routine task. This is one of the things that makes co-working and collaboration so full of possibility, and potentially so rewarding. The energy and intellectual stimulation

---

15 Blanchard, K., Bowles, S., Carew, D. and Parisi-Carew, E. (2001) *High Five! The Magic of Working Together*. New York: William Morrow.

16 Gorgenyi, I. (1998) 'Hunting territory: the structure of team life.' *Sports Coach, Summer issue*, 18–21. Available at http://huntingterritory.com/articles/HT_article01.pdf, accessed on 26 September 2013.

generated when colleagues come together around work tasks can often lead to unanticipated insights and transformational leaps forward. Teams large and small can be tremendous hubs of innovation and creativity. I was mindful of this recently when Marissa Mayer, the newly appointed Chief Executive of Yahoo!, issued the controversial directive to her thousands of employees that they must come into the office rather than work from home.[17] There was a lot of resistance to this, and a great deal of media coverage. Weren't we supposed to be moving at light speed towards the era of tele-commuting, and isn't an internet corporation ideally placed to take advantage of the technology to allow people to work from home? Mayer was clear in her rationale: employees need to work together and be in close proximity to do their most innovative work. Productivity may increase when working from home, but not innovation. For that, you need to be in close contact with colleagues. Mayer's landmark directive comes at a pivotal moment in the evolution of technology-based communication. As technology improves, it may be that Mayer's concerns will be addressed through technological innovation. For now, actual face-time still counts.

Co-creativity and innovation

However long a certain job has been done or a task undertaken, there is usually the possibility of doing it in a different way, no matter how small the difference. This is the principle of constant improvement, and it is the direct opposite of doing things by tradition, that is 'we do it this way because we have always done it this way'. And while a particular innovation may seem small or hardly worth mentioning, even in finely honed systems such as cycle racing and Formula One racing, small incremental improvements can aggregate into major triumphs.[18] Creativity and innovation can be large or small in scale, but just as important in terms of results.

17   Miller, C.C. and Rampell, C. (2013, February 25) 'Yahoo orders home workers back to the office'. *New York Times*. Available at www.nytimes.com/2013/02/26/technology/ yahoo-orders-home-workers-back-to-the-office.html?pagewanted=all, accessed 12 October 2013.

18   Peck, T. (2012, August 4) 'Dave Brailsford: Cycling coach reveals secrets to GB's success.' *The Independent*. Available at www.independent.co.uk/news/people/profiles/dave- brailsford-cycling-coach-reveals-secrets-to-gbs-success-8005870.html, accessed on 12 October 2013.

Mindful co-working starts at the top

In organizations large or small, if mindful co-working is to become embedded as a way of working, it has to start at the top. Only then will the message be received with integrity through the chain of command. How does the leadership team collaborate? How do they talk to each other? By extension, how then does the leadership team communicate with the middle management, and how in turn does middle management communicate with the front-line staff? With the answers to these questions in mind, we can then explore how ways of internal communication may then be transmitted through to the customers or clients. There is a powerful cascade effect in most organizations, particularly those where customer service is important. The way that employees and middle managers are treated will have powerful implications for the way that customers are treated.

Thinking about this idea of leading from the top, I recall a compelling occasion at the start of the US President Barack Obama's administration in 2009. Just two days after the inauguration, First Lady Michelle Obama arranged a structured meet-and-greet at the White House, where her incoming staff of advisors met the permanent White House staff such as the gardeners, the plumbers, the electricians, the catering staff and the other workers based at the White House. Some of these workers had served at the White House for decades, and some of them had postponed retirement in order to serve during the administration of the first African-American president. Michelle Obama made an impressive opening statement. She reminded the incoming workers that the permanent White House staff members were there before the Obama administration moved in and they would be there long after their administration ended. She told her advisors, 'I want you to know that you won't be judged based on whether they know your name, you'll be judged based on whether you know theirs.'[19] The message was clear: *we are not here to lord it over these people.* The two groups formed concentric circles and for an hour or so they made sure that everyone had a chance to meet and learn a little bit about each other. It was a

---

19   Gibbs, N. and Scherer, M. (2009, May 21) 'The Meaning of Michelle Obama.' *Time.* Available at http://content.time.com/time/magazine/article/0,9171,1900228,00. html, accessed on 12 October 2013.

powerful egalitarian message of solidarity and respect, for all levels of staff. It was the sort of leadership and role modelling for which Michelle Obama has become well known: humble, grateful and emphasizing the value of all service we all do for each other. Her approach serves well as a model for any leader looking to set the right tone for mindful co-working in their organization. It is also the kind of intervention that can make any organization a place where people love to work.

Questions to consider:

- How important is close co-working in your workplace or in your occupation?
- How inter-dependent are you on collaboration with colleagues?
- How accountable are you for your actions in the workplace? How do you share accountability with colleagues? Similarly, how much responsibility do you have for completing work tasks? How is responsibility shared with colleagues?
- What is the role of team playing in your organization? Do people work in sub-units, working parties and teams? How well do these function? What would enhance their functioning?
- How creative is your co-working? Are there any recent examples you can think of where colleagues developed an innovation in your workplace – however large or small?
- How well does the leadership team model mindful co-working? Do the leaders in this organization practise what they preach in terms of mindful communication?
- Do you know the first names of the people in your organization who work in the lower status jobs? What difference might it make if you were to make more of an effort to communicate mindfully with all grades of staff?

FIFTH PRINCIPLE: MINDFUL CO-WORKERS HELP EACH OTHER TO DEVELOP, AND THEY RELY ON EACH OTHER TO IMPROVE THE CO-WORKING RELATIONSHIP

This principle speaks to the crucial role that co-workers have in helping each other to develop as workers, with increasing skills, knowledge, confidence and effectiveness. It also affirms that co-workers themselves have a crucial role to play in the quality and improvement of their co-working relationships.

Why is this principle so important? In most cases, there is a lot to learn from your colleagues. Perhaps one of your co-workers has far greater experience in a given task. Or maybe someone else has crucial knowledge about a certain area of the work. Maybe another co-worker has skills, qualities or innovative capacities that you are still developing. If you approach your colleagues with the attitude of genuine openness to and interest in their skills, knowledge and feedback, there is no limit to the amount of professional expertise that can be honed and knowledge gained from colleagues.

A neglected principle

The fifth principle is probably the least understood and most often overlooked. The reason for this is probably that most people think that they should do most of their learning by attending education and training classes, receiving on-the-job training from people with the trainer or mentor role, or should learn it themselves through trial and error. This loses sight of the fact that most people work much more closely and for far longer with their immediate colleagues than they spend attending classes or receiving on-the-job training or supervision.

Another possibility is that, in some organizations, co-workers are seen mainly as competitors to be trodden on while grasping the greasy pole of career advancement. While this may be a reality in some organizations and professions, this book offers an alternative view, which is that when co-workers help each other to develop, the whole organization thrives and everyone advances together. Where *mindful co-working* permeates an organization, workers who operate together on a win-win basis will be the workers who advance. This is because mindful supervisors and managers know greasy-pole behaviour and one-upmanship when they see it, they know how to look for it, and they know to promote workers who are invested in the whole organization and a win-win paradigm.

Competitiveness and the win-win paradigm

Competitiveness is not a bad word among colleagues. Indeed, healthy competition can bring needed energy into a co-working situation. However, competitive spirits must be channelled with intelligence and care; they can easily tip over into sharp-elbowed behaviour that destroys trust and good will among co-workers. This is a fragile balance, and to help get the balance right it may help to spend a moment looking at the spectrum of exchange among humans – a spectrum of behaviour that we share with all animals.

The spectrum of exchange is a way of understanding the give and take of interactions among animals. In humans and, to some degree, in other higher primates, exchange becomes conscious, which is to say that we think about what to give and what to take, and we can vary our approach depending on circumstances and based on prior learning and experimentation.

Sennett describes a spectrum of five types of exchange, from the altruistic through to the viciously competitive.[20] The five types are:

1. *Altruism:* This is where you sacrifice yourself to the other person or to the greater good of the organization or the cause. There is usually a strong internal motivation to do the right thing, a striving for balance, or justice, or progress – but not for praise, advancement or personal recognition. Examples include the person who takes on enormous responsibilities and workload, works extremely long hours or completes tasks that others have not or with a dedication and attention to detail far and above the call of duty. History offers heroic examples of self-sacrifice, for example in Joan of Arc, or countless tales of war-time heroism and self-sacrifice where soldiers dive on a grenade, storm a gun position or draw fire to protect their fellow soldiers. Altruism often springs from a deep desire to help. In the workplace, the risk is that interactions and contributions may become unbalanced among co-workers. Or, the self-sacrificing worker may burn themselves out and inadvertently take down others with them.

2. *Win-win:* In a win-win exchange, you and the other person benefit from the exchange. On an organizational level, it means that different teams, departments or sections work

---

20 Sennett, R. (2012) *Together: Rituals, Pleasures and Politics of Cooperation.* London: Penguin, pp.72–85.

together so that the whole organization succeeds. This
is the desired position in mindful co-working, where all
parties collaborate for their mutual benefit and for the
benefit of the organization and the people they serve.

The archetype of the win-win exchange is the business
deal where all parties gain from the exchange. The
exchange is reciprocal and all parties are overtly aware
of this. In the workplace, in a win-win situation you and
your colleagues all look good, and you mutually strive
to make each other look good and to share the credit
when things go well, and accountability when things go
badly. As work progresses, colleagues work in attuned
and dynamic ways, playing to each others' strengths and
shoring up weaknesses as needed. When mistakes happen,
responsibility is shared, because colleagues in a win-win
exchange understand that they work within a system, and
when mistakes occur the system itself may need to change,
not just individuals within the system.

3. *Differentiating exchange:* Differentiating exchanges are where
    people discover and define the boundaries between them.
    It is the province of the full-and-frank discussion and
    the airing of differences. It is the type of process where
    intelligent adults, after full debate, may agree to disagree
    and either go their own ways or agree to collaborate with
    an understanding that in some areas they may never agree.
    In international relations, it is the exchange of 'détente' or
    of peaceful coexistence. It is the absence of war rather than
    the rich and sustained enjoyment of collaborative human
    exchange.

    Co-working and collaboration can still exist in this
    zone of exchange, but it will never be as smooth as
    win-win exchange unless there are deliberate and sensitive
    attempts built into the exchange which build bridges
    and help all parties feel valued, equal and respected. To
    offer an example of such bridge-building, as a college
    student I worked several summers in a large international
    call centre with employees from a wide range of national
    backgrounds, many of whom were immigrants specifically

hired because of their language skills. The managers made a special point of including large banners with welcoming messages in scores of different languages related to the employees' countries of origin. They combined this with culturally varied cuisine in the canteen, celebration of different national traditions, and places where people could post photos and artefacts from their home countries. They also made a point of actively seeking out and promoting staff from as wide a variety of national backgrounds as possible. They saw this as one of their strengths as an organization. All of these activities and processes served to mitigate potential cultural conflicts and to increase cultural awareness and respect. Differences were welcomed and not treated as obstacles to co-working. It worked well, and I recall being impressed by the international feeling of the place and the managers' efforts to make it a welcoming, constructive place to work.

4. *Zero-sum:* This is where you win and the other person loses – or vice versa. This is a very common form of exchange in modern, competitive societies. In the workplace, it manifests in greasy-pole politics where co-workers compete for promotion. In the classroom, testing usually demarcates winners and losers. On the sports field, winning and losing is the name of the game. And in the financial markets, where the principle of buy low and sell high is the prime directive, one person's monetary gain is usually another's loss. Translated to the co-working environment, in this paradigm the sharp-elbowed and ruthless will advance and the gullible or sensitive will be left behind. It makes for great television drama, but if you work in such an environment it's hell to live through.

5. *Winner-takes-all:* This is where you win and the other person is destroyed. It is the law of the jungle – Hobbes' view of nature, red in tooth and claw. This is the logic of predator-prey, slash-and-burn, of total war, of genocide. As a species, we still have this propensity, as is made clear in the headlines every day. Equally, we have the capacity

to eradicate this form of exchange, and the optimistic view of humanity is that we may well manage it as a species as we become steadily more integrated, more democratic and more aware of how to manage our inner landscapes.

While the workplace may seem an unlikely place for such annihilating instincts as winner-takes-all to manifest themselves, any high octane workplace may succumb, and in times of great uncertainty and upheaval, the winner-takes-all strategy may feel instinctively appealing. It speaks to the most basic and ruthless instincts to survive, and when it feels one's life or livelihood is in danger, it is a strategy that may feel adaptive to the context. It is best to remember, in such instances, that the instinct to annihilate the other is driven by fear untempered by reason. In such situations, pause for reflection is called for, and good advice from a trusted mentor or outside source. Remember the Confucian adage: *Before you embark on a journey of revenge, dig two graves.*

Great expectations: developing the co-working relationship

When co-workers use a win-win approach to collaboration, an interesting possibility arises: we can take joint responsibility for developing and enhancing not just our performance as workers, but also the co-working relationship itself.

In mindful co-working, colleagues understand that the co-working relationship is an entity in itself and must be looked after; all parties have responsibility for the quality and improvement of the collaboration. Mindful co-workers understand that they can't rely solely on supervisors and managers to help them get along with each other and work effectively as a unit, so they take significant responsibility for this themselves. When there are ruptures in the co-working relationship, such as a mis-step or a disappointing interaction, all parties take equal responsibility for repairing the co-working relationship. Sometimes this is assisted or brokered, for example by a supervisor, but even in this case the parties try to work it out with each other and do not resort to telling tales or venting to third parties, that is, gossiping. Only in the worst and most intractable cases should formal grievance be needed; in organizations using mindful co-working, this should be vanishingly rare.

Looking after the co-working relationship also means that we play to each others' strengths and shore up weaknesses. If one colleague knows that their co-worker excels in a particular part of the job, it makes sense to let them carry that out. At the same time, a more able colleague can help a less able one, providing guidance and assistance in graduated stages until they are confident and skilled in the task.

When co-working relationships are functioning very well, and as the trust deepens between colleagues, the relationship becomes more robust. Co-workers feel more able actively to seek out weaknesses in the system, and the strength of the relationship allows them to reflect on opportunities to improve their work. In highly evolved co-working relationships, the co-workers are able to become, in Nicolas Taleb's phrasing, 'anti-fragile'.[21] That is to say, when trouble happens, mindful co-workers take it as a learning opportunity, process the difficulty and come back stronger than ever. Taleb uses the example of the airline industry, which grows ever safer as lessons are learned; the industry as a whole becomes stronger and safer each time something goes wrong with an aircraft. In the same way, mindful co-working relationships can become ever-stronger when co-workers take an anti-fragile approach to learning from their mis-steps.

Shared consciousness in closelyknit teams

When co-working pairs and teams start working really well together, they can become very closely integrated units. Examples of this might include a bike racing team, a tight-knit platoon out on patrol, a well-honed acrobatic troupe, or an experienced surgical team. At a certain point, their level of synchrony reaches the point where they begin to share communication on a deep and intuitive level. The level of sensitivity and intuition about each others' thoughts, feelings and actions becomes so subtle that the unit works as a unified entity

---

21   Taleb, N.N. (2012) *Antifragile: How to Live in a World We Don't Understand.* London: Allen Lane.

– almost a single organism. When co-working pairs or teams – or indeed whole organizations – work at this level, there is powerful unity of purpose and mutual support. People instinctively watch each others' backs, play to each others' strengths, and everyone is carried forward on the wave of unified intention and concentrated action.

Questions to consider:

- Can you describe the five principles of mindful co-working? What distinguishes the first three principles from principles four and five?

- How can these principles be integrated into your co-working and your organization? Would they need any adjustments?

- What do you think of the proposition contained in the fifth principle, that supervisors and managers can set the tone and provide the structure and training, but it is then up to each worker to carry out and improve their co-working relationships using the principles of mindful co-working? What are your ideas about how co-workers can develop and enhance their co-working relationships?

- More broadly, what do you think are the benefits of co-working? What about the drawbacks or potential challenges of co-working?

CHAPTER 2

The Ten Key Skills of Mindful Co-working

In this chapter, you will learn:
- the distinction between shared co-working and the lead worker/ co-worker format, and which co-working situations these modes are best suited to
- the five key skills of shared co-working and the five key skills used in the lead worker/co-worker format.

KNOWING THE 'RULES OF THE ROAD'

The most effective and enjoyable co-working happens when colleagues agree on the principles and practical techniques they will use when working together. This chapter builds on the principles from Chapter 1 and describes the specific skills and procedures for optimal co-working. Because the topics are so deeply interconnected, Chapters 1 and 2 should be read together.

Truly mindful co-working – where workers keep each other in mind with trust and respect, and constantly adjust their actions based on their understanding of each other – is like a seemingly effortless dance. Or, to use the well-known motoring analogy: In order to work well together, we all need to follow the same rules of the road. This means knowing the processes and desired outcome of the work we are doing, and also agreeing the type of co-working we will use. This is essential if colleagues are to work smoothly together and to avoid crossing into each others' lanes or metaphorically (and, in some occupations, literally) crashing into each other.

THE TWO TYPES OF CO-WORKING

This chapter describes two types of co-working, each with its own rules of engagement. Each type is appropriate to different working situations or types of process. The first five skills apply very widely to most co-working situations, and the next five are particularly relevant to situations where you are working jointly with colleagues in front of other people – for example if you are making presentations, training, facilitating groups, leading activities or running meetings.

Between them, these two modes of working cover most co-working situations. In both types of co-working, colleagues share power and authority, but this is done in different ways depending on which mode of co-working is used. In order to distinguish the two forms of co-working, they are given different names: *shared co-working* is the first type and *lead worker/co-worker* is the second.

HERE IS A QUICK REFERENCE LIST OF THE TEN SKILLS DESCRIBED IN THIS CHAPTER:

Skills of shared co-working

1. transparency
2. informal turn-taking that conveys equality
3. supporting each others' status
4. active listening
5. choosing positions that make it easy to communicate.

Skills used in the lead worker/co-worker format

1. The lead worker is the 'traffic conductor'.
2. The lead worker brings in the co-worker at regular intervals.
3. The co-worker can contribute or intervene at any time.

4. Transitions between leaders can be planned or unplanned.

5. The co-worker lends focus to the lead worker.

In general, it is counter-productive to try to mix the two types of co-working, or to leave unspecified the type you will be using, as this can lead to uncertainty and distraction, especially if colleagues have different assumptions about the type of co-working being used.

THE FIVE KEY SKILLS OF SHARED CO-WORKING

The first type of co-working is called *shared co-working*. It is used very widely and applies to paired co-working, teams, sections, departments and whole organizations.

As the name implies, in this mode of interaction the co-working is shared equally and informally, with co-workers speaking to each other and – where relevant – speaking to the participants, observers, customers or clients with no sense of one worker being the lead. Both workers equally share responsibility for the focus and effectiveness of the session or work in progress. They also share the time equally, and neither person is dominant.

Shared co-working is appropriate for many situations. It can be used in joint presentations, co-running a meeting, in general discussions or in any jointly delivered activity where there is no need for one person to take the overall lead. A good exemplar of share co-working is seen on many breakfast television news programmes, where co-presenters (usually a man and a woman) share the air time equally and informally, with no sense that one is the leader. Even though they may in fact have very different levels of seniority or status within the organization, when they are in shared co-working mode they are operating as equals.

You can also see shared co-working operating in environments where there are more than two people co-working, such as in a large and well-run office, a well-functioning sports team or an air traffic control tower. While staff hierarchy will still be present in most organizational settings, when shared co-working is in operation, people's rank or status takes second place to the smooth operating principles of shared co-working.

SHARED CO-WORKING SKILL
NUMBER ONE: TRANSPARENCY

In mindful co-working, colleagues try to be as transparent as possible in sharing their thinking with each other. This also applies if there are other people present, such as clients, participants, patients or customers.

Examples include:

A group of workers is on a building site, making a constant series of suggestions and adjustments as they manoeuvre a piece of equipment into a tight spot.

A surgical team is performing an operation, with different members of the team speaking as their role and responsibilities require, checking and ensuring the safety and effectiveness of the procedure.

Two co-presenters are leading a session, with each speaking to the other as they make decisions and adjustments as they proceed. When one presenter makes a suggestion to move in a new direction, they share this suggestion and the reason for it with their co-worker, in front of and within the hearing of the people they are presenting to or working with.

When colleagues use this degree of transparency, they convey a deep level of respect for each other and also – where relevant – for the clients, participants or audience. Being transparent and clear with each other makes it much less likely that there will be controversy or friction between the co-workers and between the workers and the participants, because people will understand the decisions being made and the purposes of each task they are involved in.

Transparency is also important because in shared co-working all workers are equally and jointly responsible for carrying out their tasks. A co-worker cannot simply let their co-worker carry on the exercise or task if he or she is getting into danger, deviating significantly from the aims of the work or working outside professional norms and standards. Using the skill of transparency, a co-worker can speak freely and openly, without resorting to hand signals, urgent facial expressions or ambiguous throat clearing noises. How refreshing to know that you can actually speak to each other.

Reflection: How would this co-working skill apply to my occupation, role or work setting?

SHARED CO-WORKING SKILL NUMBER TWO: INFORMAL TURN-TAKING THAT CONVEYS EQUALITY

The second skill of shared co-working is the skill of informal turn-taking that conveys equality. This skill, when performed with integrity, offers a strong message of shared power and authority, and respect for each person's role and importance to the organization and the task, regardless of rank or seniority.

When used as intended, this skill helps to ensure that colleagues perform as equals during the session. This skill is especially relevant even when a senior colleague is co-working with someone of lower power status in the organization. At a meeting of the board of directors in a large company, the chair is co-working with the junior secretary who is taking the minutes of the meeting just as much as he or she is co-working with fellow members of the board.

You could argue that mindful co-working is even more important when there are vast differences in power and status, because the person of higher rank can so easily forget or overlook the common humanity they share with people of lower status. We are all too familiar with endless stories of workplace bullying and harassment from higher to lower ranking staff (which is not to ignore harassment among staff of equal rank).

Example from a meeting

Senior manager to junior worker: James, I notice (X), and I wonder if you think it might be the right time to discuss (Y)? I could speak about that and give people the context?

Junior worker: Thanks very much, Hilary. I agree, and that's a helpful suggestion. Let's move on to (Y) and I'll hand over to you, Hilary.

Or the roles could be reversed:

Junior worker to senior manager: Hilary, I am aware that (X) and I wonder what thoughts you have about addressing (Y) at this point? I could speak about that and give people the context?

Senior manager: Thanks very much, James. Your timing is excellent and I agree we should bring in (Y) now. Can you bring us up to speed?

Example from a co-presentation

Rachel and Matt are at the front of the room, leading a discussion during a training event. They sit side by side, and speak to the group and to each other. They play equal roles in facilitating the discussion, and smoothly 'pass the baton' back and forth while asking questions, clarifying points, imparting information, summarizing learning and moving the discussion on. They are mindful of sharing the time and focus equally, and actively demonstrate that they value each others' thoughts and contributions. They share the responsibilities equally, and there is no sense of one or the other being a lead worker or senior partner.

Dynamic duos in software engineering

In the field of software development, a tried and tested method of shared co-working is known as *paired programming*. In this method, two software designers sit side by side, with one person – known as the 'driver' – taking primary responsibility for writing computer code, while the other person – the 'navigator' – checks each line of code as it is typed in. The navigator keeps an eye on overall strategy and makes notes of possible bugs or inconsistencies that will need checking. The two people frequently switch roles in order to provide variety and keep the process fresh. When paired programming is working well, the software code that results typically has between 15–50 per cent fewer defects (bugs), depending on the experience levels of the programmers, how well they work as a team, and the complexity of the task.[1]

Here is a very telling excerpt that captures an important benefit of pairing more experienced and less experienced staff together. Although it is drawn from the field of software development, it could apply in almost any occupation:

> I was sitting with one of the least-experienced developers, working on some fairly straightforward task. Frankly, I was thinking to myself that with my great skill in Smalltalk [a programming language], I would soon be teaching this young programmer how it's really done.
>
> We hadn't been programming more than a few minutes when the youngster asked me why I was doing what I was doing. Sure enough, I was off on a bad track. I went another way. Then the whippersnapper reminded me of the correct method name for whatever I was mistyping at the time. Pretty

---

1   Cockburn, A. and Williams, L. (2000) 'The Costs and Benefits of Pair Programming.' Proceedings of the First International Conference on Extreme Programming and Flexible Processes in Software Engineering (XP2000).

soon, he was suggesting what I should do next, meanwhile calling out my every formatting error and syntax mistake. I'm not entirely stupid. I noticed very quickly that this most junior of programmers was actually helping me. Me! Can you believe it? Me! That has been my experience every time thereafter, in pair-programming. (Ron Jeffries, p.1)[2]

Reflection: How would this co-working skill apply to my occupation, role and work setting?

SHARED CO-WORKING SKILL NUMBER THREE: CO-WORKERS SUPPORT EACH OTHERS' STATUS AND PROFESSIONALISM

The third skill of shared co-working is that co-workers find ways to support each others' status and professionalism. The idea with this skill is that both co-workers can fit in subtle reminders and embedded references to the professionalism, dedication and competence of their co-worker. This is a relatively subtle skill, but when put into practice it can have powerful effects because it enhances the rapport of the co-workers and will also increase their credibility with participants, clients or customers.

In the following example, Andrea has become aware that her co-worker Bill has missed out an important step in a task. Andrea reminds Bill of the step while at the same time reinforcing his stature, knowledge and competence:

Andrea: (smiling, confident and clear) Bill, I recall that in our planning session, you spoke about how important it was for our colleagues to be aware of (topic or procedure). I wonder if you think now might be a good time to introduce that concept?

Bill: (appreciative, open and grateful) Thank you very much for that reminder, Andrea. It is important to make people aware of that, and we can go on to cover that now.

Notice how Andrea subtly reinforces Bill's competence when she refers to his comments during the planning session. This is

---

2   Jeffries, R. 'A First Pair-programming Experience.' In Williams, L. Jeffries, R. and Kessler, R.R. *Strengthening the Case for Pair-Programming.* Available at www.cs.utah.edu/~lwilliam/Papers/ieeeSoftware, accessed on 26 September 2013.

important, because her reminder could be seen by the observers as undermining Bill's authority and knowledge.

It is also worth noticing that, in this example, Bill does not become embarrassed and apologetic. Nor does he become defensive or snap back at Andrea that he 'knew that and was about to cover that anyway'. The approach is instead one of constant support and mindful, pro-social working together.

Congruence

While they are co-working, it is important for colleagues to convey mutual appreciation and respect not only in what they say but how they say it. To put this another way, verbal and non-verbal communication should be *congruent*. Otherwise, serious damage can be done to the co-working relationship, and the work or task will be adversely affected. So in the example above, when Bill thanks Andrea, his thanks are not offered in rote fashion; he really appreciates her intervention and he wants her to know how grateful he is to be working with her and to have her eyes on the effective delivery of their work together. Because he feels this genuinely, his thanks are genuine, and they sound genuine.

There is another compelling reason why communication needs to be congruent. In situations where co-workers are leading a meeting or a presentation, if the co-workers appear to be at odds, this is distracting for onlookers. Because of our evolutionary need to understand status within the group, humans are wired to try to figure out the relationships between other people. So when we see co-workers who have an uneven approach, we find ourselves wondering 'Who's in charge?' 'Do they like each other?' So don't let poor co-working become the main event.

> *Reflection:* How would this co-working skill apply to my occupation, role and work setting?

SHARED CO-WORKING SKILL NUMBER FOUR: CO-WORKERS USE ACTIVE LISTENING SKILLS TO ATTUNE WITH EACH OTHER AND THE CUSTOMERS, CLIENTS OR PARTICIPANTS

The fourth shared co-working skill is the skill of active listening in order to attune with your colleagues and the people you are working with, for example clients, customers or participants. This seems like an obvious point, but it often goes wrong without deliberate and conscious attention.

To perform this skill well, co-workers should use the same skills of active listening and mindful interaction with each other as they would with participants, clients, customers, patients or service users. Where practicable, they should listen to each other and look at each other when they are speaking. Active listening also includes verbal and non-verbal communication, and includes activities such as checking understanding, repeating to clarify, summarising, and validating what has been heard.

Exercise

Here is an active listening technique to try: In conversation, when the other person makes a statement or asks a question that requires a considered reply, pause for at least three seconds, clarify what you have heard (repeat the process if the other person clarifies what they have said) then pause again and reply.

This seemingly simple technique has the power to transform the tenor and effectiveness of spoken communication throughout an organization, especially when the leadership and senior managers take this approach with each other and with their staff teams. At the very least, it stops people talking over each other. When used with integrity and consistency, this technique rapidly boosts mutual understanding and the degree to which people feel heard and respected.

Reflection: How would this co-working skill apply to my occupation, role and work setting?

SHARED CO-WORKING SKILL NUMBER FIVE: CO-WORKERS POSITION THEMSELVES TO BE ABLE TO SEE EACH OTHER AND COMMUNICATE EASILY

In general, co-workers should be in clear view of each other. If seated around a table, they might, for example, position themselves on opposite sides of the table. In some circumstances, this will be impractical, and the co-workers may decide to sit next to each other. In this case, there would need to be enough space between them so they can turn to look at each other. It would also help if the table is round or curved, which will help the co-workers (and their participants, clients or colleagues) to see each other.

If two co-workers are leading a group and the group is seated in a semi-circle, we suggest that, in general, the two workers sit at the two ends of the semi-circle. In this way, they will serve as anchors at the ends of the group, which conveys a sense of boundaries and safety for the participants. There are times when co-workers choose to sit randomly among a seated group of participants. Wherever they sit, group leadership should be transparent and clear.

A word about technical equipment and visual aids: If you and your co-worker plan to use projectors, flipcharts or other equipment or visual aids, you will need to plan ahead so you can use these while also being able to see each other easily. If the participants will be moving (for example, if you will be facilitating role plays or active exercises), you will also need to plan where you will position yourselves during the exercise or task.

Reflection: How would this co-working skill apply to my occupation, role or work setting?

THE FIVE KEY SKILLS FOR USING THE LEAD WORKER / CO-WORKER FORMAT

The second type of co-working is called the *lead worker/co-worker* format. In the lead worker/co-worker format, each co-worker is at various times in the role of lead worker or co-worker, and they usually maintain these roles for the duration of a complete exercise or task.

This is a style of co-working that seems deceptively simple, but it has some subtle and important skills underlying it which need to be followed in order for the process to work as intended. The lead worker/co-worker format, above all other concepts in the mindful approach to co-working, is the most likely to be misunderstood or mishandled. When it is done well, however, it is a very positive and effective co-working arrangement. So please take your time getting to grips with these five skills, even if you read the rest of the book at speed.

WHERE THE LEAD WORKER/CO-WORKER FORMAT IS BEST SUITED

The lead worker/co-worker format is appropriate for a wide range of work activities, including:

- where a complex, high-intensity task is undertaken – examples include a patient or client interview, a consultation, a formal hearing, a medical procedure, flying an aircraft, policing a crime scene, putting out a fire or piloting a boat

- where colleagues have different levels of experience, the more experienced colleague can take the lead to model the skill or process, with support from the less experienced person – alternatively, the less experienced colleague can take the lead, with support from the more experienced person

- co-chairing meetings

- co-delivering presentations

- co-leading groups of all types

- when co-workers are leading any active or experiential exercise – this might include group-building exercises, energizers, role play, problem-solving tasks or theme-focused experiential exercises

- co-leading sports and adventure-based activities

- in group work settings, this format of co-working is also needed when one participant, client or patient is in the spotlight for a significant period of time, for example if they are doing a focused piece of work in front of the group: the lead worker/co-worker format is best in these situations because you need one worker to concentrate on the person in focus, while the other worker concentrates on making sure that the rest of the group stay involved (the other benefit is that the person in focus only needs to respond to one worker; it can get confusing for them otherwise, especially when they are facing the anxiety of being in focus in front of a group of people)

- in group work, this format for co-working can also be used, as an option, during general group discussion – for example, if you and your co-worker decide that the group needs strong leadership from a single worker, with the other worker offering support, then you would use the lead worker/co-worker format.

LEAD WORKER/CO-WORKER SKILL NUMBER ONE: THE LEAD WORKER IS THE 'TRAFFIC CONDUCTOR' FOR THE ACTIVITY, AND THE CO-WORKER'S CONTRIBUTIONS GO THROUGH THE LEAD WORKER

In this type of co-working, the lead worker is, in effect, the traffic conductor for the task or activity being undertaken. He or she is the traffic conductor in the sense that all interventions, suggestions, questions and interactions suggested by the co-worker are first directed to the lead worker. The lead worker can then decide to take on the suggestion offered or may decide to address it in another way or at another time.

Here is an example:

During a presentation, the co-worker (in this case, John) asks the lead worker (Karen) if she thinks it might be a good time to take questions:

CW: Karen, I can see a few people look like they might have questions about what you have just said. Might it be a good time to take questions?

The lead worker thanks the co-worker and praises his suggestion, and decides to take up the suggestion:

LW: (with genuine praise and thanks) Thanks very much, John. That's helpful. Let's take a moment to check with the group: what clarifications or further information might be helpful?

You can see here how the co-worker has offered his suggestion in the form of a question (see further information about this under skill three) and the lead worker, as traffic conductor, has taken up the suggestion.

It is equally possible that the lead worker may have a different idea about the direction to take. In the following example, the same lead worker, Karen, chooses to handle John's suggestion in a different way:

CW: Karen, I can see a few people look like they might have questions about what you have just said. Might it be a good time to take questions?

LW: (with genuine praise and thanks) Thanks very much, John. That's a useful suggestion. I think what I'll do is finish the next couple of points in the presentation, which may answer some questions. Then we can see if people need further clarification.

CW: (smiles and offers affirmative body language) Of course, Karen.

In this example, Karen decides that it is best to carry on with the session without pausing for questions. John agrees with Karen, and the session proceeds. To explain this a little further, the lead worker, as traffic conductor, has the prerogative of deciding whether or not to take the co-worker's suggestion. Crucially, however, this 'rule of the road' applies only as long as the decision of the lead worker *adheres to the structure and intent of the task or exercise and the common safety and working practices of their profession.* As long as this is the case, the co-worker *defers* to the lead worker's decision even if the co-worker thinks they would themselves handle it in a different way. In the example, Karen is adhering to the structure and intent of the presentation and is working within the common principles of their profession. She is simply making a different – but nevertheless valid – judgement call. The co-worker does not force the issue or convey his disappointment or chagrin during the session. If it seems important enough, the co-worker may choose to raise the issue during the de-brief session, to check out what the lead worker's thinking was at the time.

Note: You may also notice how John has used the skill of *transparency* in this example, by explicitly stating the reasons he is offering his suggestion. This shows how the various skills can be used in combination, often simultaneously.

A crucial caveat, about safety and ethics

However, if the lead worker's decision to carry on is dangerous or represents a breach of professional ethics or runs another form of significant risk, the co-worker has the authority to intervene more strongly, including calling a halt to the activity or taking a time out to ensure safety and ethical boundaries are maintained. The co-worker does not abdicate responsibility simply because there is a lead worker.

To offer perhaps the most harrowing example of this principle going wrong, in March 1977 on Tenerife, in the Canary Islands, 583 passengers were killed when two planes collided on the runway in heavy fog.[3] Examination of the cockpit voice recorder of the plane that was at fault found that the First Officer and Flight Engineer – who both appeared uncertain about whether another plane had cleared the runway – both deferred to the pilot at the crucial moment when the pilot began take-off, despite the control tower not having given clearance. In the heavy fog, they could not see that another plane was taxiing across the runway as they were speeding towards take-off. The planes collided on the runway. The First Officer and Flight Engineer, in deferring to their senior colleague, abdicated their equal responsibility for safety, and hundreds died as a result. This disaster, and a number of other disasters caused when subordinate crew members deferred to senior colleagues, led to a shift in training not only in the airline industry but also in military, fire and disaster services. The new system, originating at NASA and known as *crew resource management*,[4] is specifically designed to counteract hierarchies in order to include the broadest range of ideas among crew and team members in high pressure occupations. Here's how it might sound in a fire service or airline situation:[5]

- *Get the person's attention:* 'Hey Sarge', or 'Captain Jones', or 'Dave'. Use a name or title that will get the person's attention in the right way. Be clear and direct; you don't need to apologize if you are calling something important to their attention.

- *State your concern:* Give your assessment of the situation in a clear and direct manner. Refer to your own feelings about

---

3   This was the worst airline accident in history, in terms of fatalities. See Krock, L. (2006) *The Final Eight Minutes*. Available at www.pbs.org/wgbh/nova/space/final-eight-minutes.html, accessed on 26 September 2013.

4   Cooper, G.E., White, M.D. and Lauber, J.K. (eds) (1980) 'Resource management on the flight deck.' Proceedings of a NASA/Industry Workshop (NASA CP-2120).

5   International Association of Fire Chiefs (2003) *Crew Resource Management: A Positive Change for the Fire Service*. Fairfax, VA: International Association of Fire Chiefs.

the situation if this will help. 'If we attempt to fly around that storm system, my concern is that we don't have enough fuel.' 'I'm worried that roof is going to collapse.'

- *State the problem as you see it:* 'We have 50 minutes of fuel left.' 'There's evidence of fire in the roof structure, and the truss system is likely to be weakened.'

- *State a solution:* 'I think we should divert to the nearest airport and refuel.' 'Why don't we pull back some of the tiles and have a look with thermal imaging before we send anyone inside?'

- *Obtain agreement (or buy-in):* This is usually best phrased in the form of a question, leaving the other person options but also making it clear that a decision is needed. 'What do you think, boss?'[6]

In even more urgent situations, where time is extremely limited and the danger appears imminent, workers can leave aside discussion and call for a time out. When a lead worker or co-worker calls time out, this is never overridden by the other worker. There may be exceptions to this rule in situations of war, policing and emergencies, but the circumstances are rare indeed in which a leader should override the safety concerns of colleagues where life and limb are at stake.

Reflection: What would be an example of this skill in my occupation, role or work setting?

LEAD WORKER/CO-WORKER SKILL NUMBER TWO: THE LEAD WORKER BRINGS IN THE CO-WORKER AT REGULAR INTERVALS

The second lead worker/co-worker skill is that the lead worker should turn at regular intervals to the co-worker to invite their contribution.

Here are some examples:

---

6   This example is adapted from an example shown at http://en.wikipedia.org/wiki/ Crew_resource_management, accessed on 15 April 2013.

Lead worker: Marie, did you want to add anything at this point? In particular, I would be interested in your views about (Y) because I know you have a unique role in relation to this issue.

or

Lead worker: (After fielding a question from the audience) Marie, in reply to (X's) question, I know this is an area in which you have particular skill and experience. Can I bring you in at this point for any thoughts you have about her question?

This skill can be a real challenge for lead workers who are not used to co-working, or who work under the misapprehension that being the lead worker means 'I must do it all myself'. However, if the lead worker uses this technique, they make the process of facilitation or presentation much smoother, because the co-worker does not have to try to 'break in' to be heard. The co-worker can be confident that, at regular intervals, the lead worker will turn to them and ask for a question, comment or other contribution.

Lead workers who develop this skill will greatly enhance their effectiveness, because the entire process of co-working will be enhanced. Both workers can relax and be assured of mutual support and equal participation.

Reflection: What would be an example of this skill in my occupation, role or work setting?

LEAD WORKER/CO-WORKER SKILL NUMBER THREE: THE CO-WORKER CAN INTERVENE AT ANY TIME, AND SHOULD GENERALLY DO THIS IN THE FORM OF A QUESTION

At any point during a session, the co-worker can intervene, make suggestions or otherwise contribute. There is a balance to be struck, however, because too much intervention will be disruptive to the lead worker/co-worker process. So interventions must be well-judged and mindful.

The co-worker's interventions are best done in the form of a question, because a question gives the lead worker options. Having options is necessary if the lead worker is to carry out their role as traffic conductor (see above).

Why might a co-worker intervene? There are many possible reasons. For example, the co-worker may simply have an additional point to make which has not yet been covered, or they may have noticed something happening in the group that the lead worker has not seen. Or, the co-worker might hear their colleague giving incorrect information, missing important information, or getting into a 'head to head' argument with a participant, client or customer. In such instances, it is important that the co-worker positively intervenes and brings the session or the task back on course.

Here are some examples:

Co-worker to lead worker: Elizabeth, I noticed that a few people are raising their hands. I wonder if you think this would be a good time to pause for questions?

or

Co-worker to lead worker: David, before we move on to the next step, might this be a good time to try (X)?

or

Co-worker to lead worker: (Seeing that the lead worker has become verbally entangled with a participant who is dominating the group or audience) Sarah, I am aware that the topic Roger is raising is one that other people have mentioned. What if we make a note of the issue and come back to it later, after you and I have had time to discuss any adjustments we might need to make. What do you think?

LW: Thanks, Howard. That's helpful. Howard, would you please make a note of that and we can come back to your point later in the day, Roger. Let's return to the presentation…

In each of these examples, the co-worker is clearly maintaining a co-leadership role, but they are doing so while also preserving their colleague's role as the person making the final judgement call. Using this approach, it is possible for a co-worker to fill in any gaps that the lead worker might otherwise leave. Likewise, the co-worker may alert the lead worker to changing dynamics among the group/ audience/clients, and offer suggestions about ways to alleviate any problems arising. In this way, they are helping to lighten the load carried by the lead worker.

It is also worth noting that this technique is a powerful yet subtle way for more experienced workers to offer support to new or less experienced colleagues. Imagine, in the above examples, if the co-worker was actually the more senior colleague.

This approach can also be used in live mentoring, for example when the mentor or coach intervenes by asking a question of the person they are coaching.

Here is an example:

Mentor/coach to lead worker: Gerry, I notice that you are doing (X). I wonder if you thought at this point about (Y) or (Z)? What do you think?

Thanking your co-worker, even when you don't need their help

The lead worker is open at all times to questions and interventions from the co-worker, and thanks the co-worker. This would seem to be an obvious point, but I have seen it go wrong many times. The lead worker does not have to do it all. That would be a misunderstanding of the role. Instead, as traffic conductor, the lead worker has responsibility for the pace and flow of the session or task. To do this job well, the lead worker needs the co-worker, so he or she needs to show appreciation for all of the co-worker's contributions no matter what their differences are in experience or rank. (This applies even if the contribution is obvious or not particularly helpful.)

Here is an example:

CW: Annette, I know that in our planning we said we wanted to allow 30 minutes for the next activity. Do you think now would be a good opportunity to move on to (Z)?

LW: (Who was about to move on to do (Z) anyway. Showing thanks and genuine appreciation for CW's suggestion): Stephen, we're obviously on the same wavelength, because I was thinking the same thing. Thanks very much. Let's move on to do that now…

A common misunderstanding

There is sometimes a misunderstanding that *lead worker* means 'boss' and *co-worker* means 'subordinate'. This is not the case at all and is a complete misunderstanding of the intent of the lead worker/co-worker format. The co-worker is not an underling who needs permission to speak. Moreover, the co-worker never needs to apologize for speaking or making a contribution. This would set up a power imbalance and would go against the principles of co-workers sharing power equally and holding joint responsibility for the work.

The co-worker has the right to contribute, add their point of view, ask questions and suggest clarifications, as long as they apply the skills and principles we describe in this chapter.

So instead of:

CW: Oh, sorry, Pam, excuse me for cutting in, but I was wondering if…

Let's hear instead a confident and steady:

CW: Pam, just to clarify, did you want people to turn to their handouts now?

Can you hear the difference? Enough said.

Reminder: If you are the lead worker and your co-worker comes in with a question or suggestion, your response is more likely to be in tune with your co-worker if you take a moment to reflect on the reasons for the intervention. Have they spotted something you missed? Are you drifting off course?

> *Reflection:* What would be an example of this skill in my occupation, role or work setting?

LEAD WORKER/CO-WORKER SKILL NUMBER FOUR: TRANSITIONS FROM ONE LEADER TO THE OTHER CAN BE PLANNED OR UNPLANNED

During the course of making a presentation or carrying out a task, the lead worker and co-worker may decide, either in advance or on the spur of the moment, to exchange roles. This can be for a brief moment or for a significant stretch of time. In either case, it is important that the transition of leadership is made clear to all.

Planned transitions

Let's look at an example of a planned transition between a lead worker and their co-worker. In this example, the two workers have agreed during their planning session to exchange roles at a certain point:

LW: Barbara, I think we have covered that topic thoroughly, so can I hand over to you for the (new topic or task)?

CW: Thanks, Neil. I agree, this would be a good time to move on to cover (new topic or task).

This is a very common type of transition, used in most lead worker/ co-worker situations. It happens every time workers plan a session and 'divvy up' who will lead which parts of the session.

Unplanned transitions – brief and more sustained

Next, here is an example of a brief, unplanned role transition, arising spontaneously in the midst of a session.

Imagine that a class or group session is underway, and Sean, the co-worker asks the lead worker (Anita) if it might be the right time to pause for questions and clarifications:

CW: Anita, might this be a good time to ask if there are any questions? I can see that one or two people look like they might need some clarification.

The lead worker thanks the co-worker and praises their suggestion, and takes up the suggestion:

LW: (smiling and genuine in her praise and thanks) Thanks very much, Sean. That's a useful suggestion. Would you like to bring in the group here and check if there are any questions or clarifications?

In this example, the lead worker has taken up the co-worker's suggestion and has also invited the co-worker to lead the questioning and clarification slot. This is an example of smoothly passing the leadership back and forth. Such a strategy also gives the lead worker, Anita, some time to collect her thoughts and make decisions about where to go next.

It is also possible to make longer unplanned transitions between the lead worker and co-worker role. If you use this approach, it is very important to be clear about what you are doing, so that you and your colleague are clear, and also your participants or observers are clear. Otherwise there could be real confusion and anxiety about who's in charge.

Here is an example of a more sustained unplanned transition.

Imagine that the two workers have agreed beforehand that, during a session, if one of them indicates that they have two or three points they wish to make, that this is a signal that it may be useful to exchange leadership roles to address those points.

CW: Beth, as you have been speaking, I have been thinking about two or three points that we could make in relation to (the topic), specifically about (states sub-topic). I wonder if now might be a good time to address these points?

LW: Thank you, Frank. That's a useful suggestion. As you've mentioned that you have two or three points to make, can I hand over to you to explain those points, and we will continue with the broader subject after that?

In some situations, when the lead worker and co-worker exchange roles, this will require them literally to exchange places. This would apply, for example, if one of them is standing up in front of a group of people, and/or using visual aids. In other situations, exchanging leadership roles will not require changing places.

In either situation, when you have made an unplanned transition, it is important for the co-worker, once they have the floor, to be disciplined about keeping to the points they have indicated they wanted to make. After the points are covered, they should hand back to the original lead worker and resume their co-worker role. If the co-worker is not disciplined about this, it will force the lead worker to remind them of the need to get back to the main topic. If you are the lead worker in this slightly uncomfortable situation, you can still be diplomatic about retrieving the leadership role. For example:

LW: (temporarily in the co-worker position): Frank, thank you for covering those important points. In the time remaining, I'd now like to return to the broader topic area, which will reinforce the points you have made.

CW: (temporarily in the lead worker role): Of course. Thanks for that reminder, Beth. I've covered the points I was meaning to.

Reflection: What would be an example of this skill in my occupation, role or work setting?

LEAD WORKER/CO-WORKER SKILL NUMBER FIVE: THE CO-WORKER LENDS FOCUS TO AND SUPPORTS THE LEAD WORKER, WHILE ALSO OBSERVING DYNAMICS AMONG PARTICIPANTS OR CLIENTS

When using the lead worker/co-worker style of co-working, each worker has different primary tasks or functions. While we understand that the lead worker is the traffic conductor for the session or task, the co-worker also has the important task of monitoring the group, audience or participants – or other tasks, depending on the work setting. The co-worker will be more able to observe the subtle signals being conveyed, and will be able to bring these to the attention of the lead worker, if necessary.

When the co-worker is not observing the group or participants, they are looking at the lead worker in order to lend focus to the lead worker. 'Lending focus' is a term that comes from the theatre, used to convey how actors look at each other on stage and guide the audience's attention to the main focus of the scene. By looking at the lead worker and lending focus to them, the co-worker is making it more likely that the participants or clients will also focus on the lead worker and the task in hand. This is because if any of the participants look at the co-worker, their eyes will tend to follow the co-worker's toward the lead worker. They will look where the co-worker is looking. This helps to maintain everyone's attention on the task in hand.

This skill also reminds us that the co-worker must not distract attention from the lead worker unless they are making an intervention or contribution of some type.

Reflection: What would be an example of this skill in my occupation, role or work setting?

Questions to consider:

- Can you name the five key skills of shared co-working?
- Can you name the five key skills of the lead worker/co-worker format?
- Where is shared co-working used?
- Where is the lead worker/co-worker format more likely to be appropriate?
- What are the benefits of having specific 'rules of the road' for co-working? How might these benefits help the co-workers? The co-working relationship? The group atmosphere and learning?
- What are the potential pitfalls or challenges of having defined skills and rules of the road for co-working?
- How would shared co-working and/or lead worker/co-worker co-working look in your work setting? If these two types of co-working are not relevant to your workplace, which skills or principles can be applied?

CHAPTER 3

Establishing Common Ground between Co-workers

Getting It Right from the Start

In this chapter, you will learn:

- the reasons for establishing common ground with new colleagues
- the important distinction between a basic assumption group and a working group
- a wide range of questions and discussion topics for co-workers to use to establish common ground with each other
- an exercise for discussing and developing co-working skills.

When colleagues join together as a pair, a team, a department or a whole organization, if they strive for mindful co-working it is important that they talk together and find common ground. This includes discussing their work-related values, practices and expectations. It also includes discussing attitudes towards collaboration and previous experiences of co-working, because the co-working relationship may be tested and co-workers need to know how to keep the relationship strong and repair any ruptures.

Finding common ground is particularly important when colleagues will be working closely together in pressured or emotionally intense situations. When emotions are running high, mindful co-working is more important than ever. This is why finding common ground is too important to put off to another day. If you want to get things right from the start and avoid many common pitfalls that plague weakly bonded co-working teams, the common ground discussions will help.

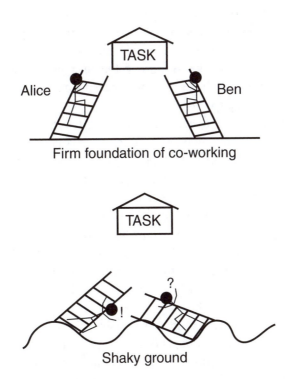

Figure 3.1: Building a co-working relationship on firm ground versus shaky ground

In this chapter, you will find a wide range of discussion topics to encourage co-workers to develop a good understanding of each other and positive rapport. For an image that captures the aim of finding common ground, see Figure 3.1. The image shows two co-workers engaged in a productive task together, safe in the knowledge that their co-working relationship is built on firm ground. By contrast, the second image shows the whole enterprise collapsing in confusion and anger when the co-working relationship is built on shaky ground.

THE DISTINCTION BETWEEN BASIC ASSUMPTION GROUPS AND WORKING GROUPS

There is a great deal of theory and research about how groups and systems function – this includes systems theory, group relations theory, sociometry, social learning theory and role theory. A particularly relevant source for us to draw upon at this point is W.R. Bion, one of the originators of group relations theory.[1] One of Bion's key observations as a group therapist and researcher into group interaction was the distinction between what he called *working groups* and *basic assumption groups.*

The working group, according to Bion, is a group where two or more people come together to accomplish a task, and they are clear about what needs to be done and their roles in relation to the task. In such situations, the people involved in the collaboration may need to question their assumptions about the task, to draw on theory, to research and find examples of similar tasks and the resulting outcomes. They may need to examine their own interpersonal process to ensure smooth communication and to enable the best ideas to emerge. In other words, they do not operate on the assumption that they are all the same or that the processes needed to accomplish their task are obvious. On the contrary, different perspectives are valued, and basic assumptions are questioned. Examples of working groups include a team of builders, engineers and architects constructing a bridge, a committee or board who are having a focused and relevant discussion about a complex topic, or a sports team mid-way through a challenging game. When a group is in *working group* mode, everyone knows what they are there to do, and they work in an optimal way. Things get done.

However, some groups never fully form into working groups, or, by contrast, some working groups can degenerate into what Bion called *basic assumption* groups. A basic assumption group

---

1   Bion, W.R. (2004) (First published 1961) *Experiences in Groups.* New York: Taylor and Francis.

is bonded not by a sense of common purpose but instead by intense emotion (which may go unnoticed or unacknowledged in the individuals) such as fear, anger, grief or a sense of righteous indignation, resentment, entitlement or injustice. At the same time as the group is operating based on these intense emotions, the members of the group also behave based on – in Bion's phrasing – 'basic assumptions' about the group and everyone's role in the group. Crucially, no one challenges or articulates these assumptions. Examples include fans at a football match screaming racist abuse at a football player, members of a team who are not doing any work but are instead gossiping and complaining about management (or, in a management team, gossiping and complaining about the workers or their superiors). This process can also happen when boards of directors of charities, organizations or companies get wrapped up in their own internal politics and lose sight of their original purpose as an executive board. In basic assumptions groups, work is done slowly, badly or not at all, and people and organizations are often damaged by the group process.

Problems arise when a working group starts behaving like a basic assumption group. This can happen to any working group, large or small, typically when the members of the group are dominated by intense emotions and do not pause to reflect and consider their underlying processes and purpose as a team. When groups are under pressure and emotions are running high, even well-functioning groups or teams can slide towards behaving like a basic assumption group. In such instances, groups of people can completely lose track of the original intent of coming together in the first place, as they squabble among themselves.

If we seek to work mindfully with each other, finding common ground at the start will serve as a good way to form and maintain a stance as a working group. People will be clear about their purpose in coming together and they will decide working practices that will help them to maintain optimal functioning as a working group.

SUGGESTED USE OF THE TOPICS

As you read the suggested topics for discussion, you may decide that you want to discuss these questions over the course of several sessions, and you can do this in any order you agree on. Co-workers often decide to discuss these topics a few at a time during their planning and de-brief sessions over a period of weeks.

Looking at the list of questions and topic areas below, choose those that you and your co-worker think are relevant to your field of work. As a suggestion, it may be useful for each of you to choose your own topics from the list independently, and then compare.

REMINDER ABOUT ACTIVE AND ATTENTIVE LISTENING

Be aware of *how* you are talking with each other about these issues, not just the content. It may be useful to remind yourself about *active listening skills*. These include non-verbals such as appropriate eye contact, nodding, smiling, positive voice tone, smooth body language, and giving other encouraging signals. Active listening also includes verbal skills such as repeating, clarifying, summarizing what your understanding is of points made, giving verbal emphasis, and fully listening to what the person is saying. Another feature of active listening is appropriate turn-taking and sharing the time equally. It's about listening mindfully, and pausing for thought and reflection before replying. It is not about taking control, or trying to impress or score points against the other person. Dogmatism and smooth co-working do not go together. Attention and eagerness to establish common ground and rapport are probably the most important key to successful and effective co-working.

To promote concentration and sensitive discussion, it helps to have a quiet room, with no telephone or other distractions, while discussing the topics in this chapter.

SETTING YOUR OWN LEVEL OF DISCLOSURE

Some of the suggested topics for discussion call for a degree of personal disclosure, and some are easier to broach than others. You are encouraged to set your own level of disclosure, as feels appropriate in your work context. As you and your colleagues get to know each other and perhaps build trust and rapport with each other, you may find that you can discuss topics at a deeper level. Having said that, there is no requirement to share more than you feel comfortable about sharing. I have seen very well-functioning co-workers who know very little about each others' lives, and I have also seen co-workers who have a very deep understanding of each others' life histories and patterns of response. Mindful co-working can happen at any level of personal disclosure, as long as there is a willingness to engage in genuine personal reflection, reflection on process issues between you as colleagues, and personal and professional growth.

A MODEST SUGGESTION

When you are getting to know a co-worker with whom you will have a sustained co-working relationship, go out for lunch together, or for a nice walk or to a beautiful park or other place you will both enjoy. It might make a nice change of setting for you to get to know each other and have a more relaxed conversation.

EXAMPLES OF DISCUSSION TOPICS
The basics

- What has brought us together as co-workers? Did we have a choice in the matter?
- What do we think about the processes that have brought us together? If we did not volunteer to work together: How can we work together to re-frame any potential ambivalence so we can work productively together as professionals?
- What motivates each of us in our work?
- What is something we each love about our job?
- How might it feel discussing our strengths and development areas with each other? Do we understand why we might need to discuss these topics?
- Are we ready, individually and as colleagues, to discuss deeper matters together, for example our feelings and

responses to the work, or our personal reflections on how the work is impacting us? What do we feel comfortable about discussing, and what would we prefer not to discuss?

- Will the organization support us by giving us the required time to build our co-working relationship? Does our organization endorse the importance of mutual understanding, smooth communication and mindful co-working?

Our accountability and responsibilities to the organization

- What is the work we are meant to accomplish together? Are there layers to this, that is, multiple or varied outcomes? Are some of these aims obvious and explicit, and some less obvious or implicit?

- What is the mandate for doing our work? Who has approved it?

- Who is supervising and managing the work? What is our understanding of how our work will be checked or audited? How will we use supervision? What issues might be best discussed in supervision?

- What are three to five key areas of debate within our profession related to the work we will be doing together? For example, are there competing theoretical models or models of practice that are still under debate in our field of work? Is the research contested? Are there innovations that are still under scrutiny or in the experimental stage? Where do our models of practice sit in relation to these innovations? Are we cutting edge, behind the times or just where we need to be? Do we agree on these questions? Is it important or necessary that we do agree? As we discuss these questions, we can see where there is common ground and decide how to deal with any differences between us. How do our ideas correspond with our organization's policies and ethos? Are there any gaps or contradictions between our preferred approach and the organization's expectations?

- What are the policies about and limits to confidentiality between co-workers in our agency/organization/ context? What is our agreement with each other about confidentiality?

Values and beliefs about co-working

- What are the advantages of co-working? What might be the benefits for each of us if we work effectively together?

- What do I honestly think about the value of co-working? Would part of me prefer to work alone? Am I more used to working on my own? How might this show itself in the co-working relationship?

- What factors do I think contribute to effective co-working? Is it possible to learn and improve co-working skills?

- What is the value of becoming conscious of our co-working and developing the skills of mindful co-working? How can we help to improve each others' performance?

- How important is trust between co-workers?

- What are our prior positive and negative experiences of co-working, both professional and personal? What made these experiences positive or negative? What was the impact, short and long term, of these experiences? How did we respond at the time to those experiences, and what did we learn? How much responsibility do we take for the success or otherwise of those co-working relationships?

- If we have already been working together for a while, how are we doing? Are we stuck in a rut? Do we need to break some patterns? How can we work together to make things better today?

- How important does each of us think it is to 'tune in' with each other? What are our beliefs about what tuning in looks and feels like? In effect, what would it mean for us really to be on the same wavelength with each other? What would that look and feel like? How can we make that happen? Do we want to make that happen?

- What are the basic assumptions we need to be aware of, that might seem to be obvious or implicit, but which we may nevertheless need to name? For example, we might make the basic assumption that we hold the same values about the work and the client group. Or about the best processes for co-working. Let's talk about these areas so we do not trip over assumptions.

Working well together

- How familiar are we with co-working? Does one of us have more co-working experience than the other? How might we need to take into account any differences in levels of co-working experience?

- What makes me think we might work really well together? What makes me think we might have difficulties? A little more challenging: What do I think *you* would say are the reasons we will work well together/have difficulties? (Compare responses.)

- What are your attitudes and beliefs about the need to plan properly together? How do you tend to plan? How shall we plan our work together? How much time shall we take to plan?

- What are the distinctions between colleagueship and friendship? Bearing these distinctions in mind, what might be the issues for planning and de-brief? What might be the pros and cons of working with a close friend as opposed to a colleague?

- What am I like as a co-worker on a good day? How about on a bad day? What do I need to be aware of and take responsibility for? How can you help me in such situations?

- A solution focused question: If we were planning, co-working and de-briefing really well, what would we be doing?

- Time: How long do we think it will take to develop a very effective and mutually enjoyable co-working relationship? How can we check in with each other to see how we are doing?

Understanding each other and respecting boundaries

Note: Remember to be mindful about personal and professional boundaries, and confidentiality, when discussing these matters:

- What are the limits of personal topics and levels of disclosure between us, for example during planning and de-brief sessions? What is the appropriate level of disclosure to expect from each other? How can we make each other aware of personal issues that are relevant (e.g. the impact of something said by a participant, or issues from our past), while still keeping within professional boundaries and the level of personal disclosure that feels comfortable for each of us?

- Is there anything else important to either of us that might impact on our co-working or professional role and conduct, for example political beliefs; experiences of oppression or being marginalized; sexuality; religious beliefs; stresses in relationships, family life or financial circumstances; work/life balance; prejudice; illness or disability; any other personal circumstances that may impact the work?

- Basic ideas of ourselves and what we need: each co-worker completes the sentences: *I am… The world is… / Life is… / People are… Therefore in order to survive/feel safe/ have a place, I must…* (after completing the sentences, compare responses).

Anti-discriminatory and non-oppressive practice issues

- What anti-discriminatory practice issues do we need to take into account when working? What issues related to discrimination, diversity and anti-discriminatory practice might arise during our planning, co-working (include interactions with participants, clients, etc.) and de-briefing? How shall we prevent this happening and manage it if it does arise?

- How can gender impact on co-working? For example, how might typical gender roles influence our behaviour as co-workers? What are some of the stereotypical roles and behaviour that people might assume for us? How can we counter these stereotypes in our planning and delivery? What might be the advantages of different gender combinations with the client group/customers? How can male and female workers address discriminatory, anti-social, sexist or abusive language/behaviour in the group? How can this be handled between us as workers? What are the sensitivities we need to be aware of around this issue?

- More generally, are there any concerns regarding our varying experience levels, or gender, racial or cultural or any other differences? For example, what are the cultural messages we have grown up with regarding help-giving, help-seeking and help-receiving? How shall we take these issues or differences into account in our planning, co-working and de-briefing?

- How shall we pre-empt 'splitting', that is, if one or more participants or clients try to turn one of us into the 'good' worker and one of us into the 'bad' worker?

- What are our attitudes towards office gossip in relation to colleagues, the organization, etc.? How would we recognize if the gossip is becoming toxic? How can we ensure that we do not engage in any form of derogatory gossip about each other?

Maintaining and developing our co-working relationship

- How and why could our co-working go wrong? How can we use our planning, our working together and our de-briefing to minimize the chances of things going wrong in our co-working relationship?

- How do I usually behave when I am angry or upset with my co-worker, or distressed about something that's happening in the session? What would be helpful from my co-worker if I give off these signals, or if I am in such a situation? (Each co-worker responds to these questions. Compare responses.)

- How shall we deal with difficulties between us? How shall we *not* deal with difficulties between us?

- What positive actions can we agree to take if one of us falls into a 'counsel of despair' or shows signs of burn-out about the work, their abilities, the organization, the participants/customers, etc.?

- How shall we clear the air if we experience difficulties or any obstacles to clear collaboration?

- How competitive are we? What are the possibilities that competition may come up in our co-working relationship? How shall we channel the competitive urge in productive ways? For example, can we both help each other to excel, and become better together? What might get in the way of our ability to channel our competitive urges productively, if we have them?

- Dealing with legacies: (*Note:* These questions examine personal topics and may not be appropriate to your work context. This is something to discuss with your co-worker and possibly your supervisor before opening up discussion around these topics.) What are our prior positive and negative experiences of sibling or family relationships that might impact on our co-working collaboration? For example, have either of us experienced damaging sibling rivalry or being cast in a disempowering or subordinate role in our family of origin? Conversely, have either of us been the 'boss' among a group of siblings? How might these experiences influence our implicit assumptions about co-working? How can we anticipate and/or cope with these possibilities in a way that enhances the co-working relationship? For example, how will we deal with the situation if we find that we are slighting each other or if we are becoming competitive with each other in front of the client/service user?

- Where relevant: What might be the advantages/ disadvantages of videoing (or otherwise recording) our planning and de-briefing sessions? Does our organization endorse such practice, and will our supervisor/mentor/ manager be willing to assist our planning and de-brief sessions by reviewing them and offering feedback? How can we help to make this happen?

Helping each other to develop as professionals

- What are our individual learning styles and how shall we take them into account? Am I more of a theorist, a pragmatist, an activist or a reflector? How about you?

- Are there any general strengths or weaknesses each of us is working on? For example, is one of us trying to work on issues of being over-controlling? Or reluctance to delegate? Or lacking confidence or being passive? Or using technical equipment/performing a procedure? Or better listening skills? Or remaining calm in difficult situations? Or presentation skills? Etc.

- How does each of us prefer to give and receive feedback? For example, does one of us like to hear feedback that is direct and to the point? What is our attitude toward receiving constructive critical feedback from a co-worker? What are the benefits and possible drawbacks of this?

Suggestion: Review with each other how each of you likes to receive feedback. Example: 'A helpful way for me to hear feedback, both positive and constructively critical, is…' (See guidance on feedback in Chapter 5 on 'De-briefing'.)

Working practices and interaction with participants/clients

- How can we best exhibit pro-social modelling as colleagues? (Note difference between male/female co-working and same gender co-working). What hidden assumptions might the client group make about co-workers' relationship to each other out of session, and how can we as co-workers ensure that appropriate and professional messages are conveyed?

- How will we model and convey unconditional positive regard for each other and for our clients/participants/customers? In other words, how will we show fundamental respect for each other and the people we are working with, that is, respect for them as human beings?

- Let's come up with a list of ten things that our clients/customers/participants will notice that will make a positive or negative impression of us and our organization in the first five minutes of interacting with us, for example: our attire, our eye contact, the way we greet and welcome them, the setup of the room, the visuals on the walls, etc. (After developing the list together): How can we make this better? What's the most important to focus on? How will we know when we are getting it right?

- How can we ensure that we give out appropriate and professional messages throughout our time working together, including what might seem like down time or backstage time (these are often the times when workers can forget their professional role and make unguarded comments).

- What messages do we intend to give with our appearance, dress and behaviour? What might be considered appropriate and inappropriate attire? What is the perceived professional attire of staff in our agency/organization?

- (Related to previous item) What messages will be conveyed if one worker is professionally attired and the other is dressed casually or inappropriately? (Another way to ask this question is: What do you want your participants/ clients to remember about you between sessions?)

- What preparation do we need for emergencies, for example if a participant is taken ill, or if there is an alarm?

- How will we adjust our facilitation for participants who are older or younger, those with mobility problems or disabilities, etc.?

Our co-working relationship in relation to our other colleagues and our supervisor

- How can we feed our discussion of these issues into discussions with our colleagues and team members? How can we share with them our positive experiences and learning points?

- How can we ensure that we as a pair or small team maintain our rapport and integration with the larger team/organization, so that we do not become a clique or exclusive? What might be the dangers if we become exclusive and too isolated in our co-working relationship?

- How can we improve the interchange of co-workers in our team and agency, so people are continually learning from each other and develop new skills?

- What issues do we need to bring to our individual and joint supervision sessions? How shall we report back and agree next steps? What do we agree to work on in the coming weeks, individually and together?

- How does our co-working relationship compare and contrast with our other co-working relationships in the organization? As we reflect on this question, is any action suggested?

*For people working directly with clients/service users/
customers/groups/participants (these topics may or
may not apply, depending on your working context)*

- What prejudices am I aware of in myself? What do we
  need to know about each others' prejudices and areas of
  cultural sensitivity?

- Is there anybody we are working with where we need to
  learn more about their cultural backgrounds in order to
  work effectively with them? (This is particularly important
  if we are working with marginalized groups.)

- What are the potential benefits of there being differences
  between us? In relation to these differences, what
  misunderstandings could occur and how could these be
  resolved?

- What impression might the participants have of each of us,
  based on occupation, role, age, appearance, socio-economic
  status, perceived race and culture, clothing, accent, gender
  or disability? What assumptions might the participants
  make based on their perceptions? How could that affect
  our interactions with them and with each other?

- How shall we join in any of the activities? Will we stay
  apart from the participants or will one or both of us join
  in? Will this vary depending on the activity?

- How will we respond to compliments from clients, and/or
  gifts from clients? What is the organization's policy about
  receiving gifts?

- How will we respond to hugs, for example at the end of
  groups? What are the issues around this, and does one of
  us feel more comfortable about this than the other(s)?

- How will we address matters if we become aware that
  a participant becomes attracted to or becomes overly
  dependent upon one or both of the co-workers?

- More generally, how will we maintain boundaries with
  clients/service users? What is appropriate to disclose to
  our participants/clients/patients/customers? (What are the

professional and organizational norms in relation to this?) What are the consequences if one of us discloses more than the other, for example if one of us discloses personal details and the other does not?

- Shall we stay with the clients during breaks? Discuss pros and cons.

- How shall we deal with threatening behaviour, including veiled threats?

Impact issues for workers

- What personal impact issues may arise in this work? What research are we aware of around this topic? Are there differences for male workers/female workers? Are there particular vulnerabilities we should be aware of, so we can best support each other?

- What are some of the resources we have available to help us cope with the impact of this work?

- Are there any kinds of issues that might be 'hot buttons' (difficult issues) for either of us? How can we help each other to manage this?

DRAW A PICTURE OF A HOUSE: A SIMPLE EXERCISE TO TRY AT THE START OF YOUR CO-WORKING RELATIONSHIP

When I am running workshops about co-working, I often use this simple exercise to get people talking about themes of collaboration, cooperation and interdependence. The exercise works best in pairs, but can be used with groups of two to six people. Above that number, sub-divide into smaller groups.

Exercise

Method: Sit next to your colleague(s) with a blank sheet of paper between you on a table. Using one pen or pencil, pass it back and forth as you each make one mark at a time, attempting to *draw a picture of a house* together. There must be no planning or discussion of any type before you begin to draw, and there must be no talking or gesturing during the process. You are simply making one mark at a time and then passing the pen or pencil to your colleague.

A 'mark' for the purposes of this exercise is a line, a curve or a circle, but nothing more. It may be tempting to do more, for example an 'L' shape, but that is too much in this exercise. Keep it to one simple mark at a time only.

As the exercise progresses, people are often delighted at how quickly the house takes shape. Sometimes quite extraordinary buildings are created, and sometimes the house that is created follows well-known patterns. Either way, there is a lot to talk about afterwards.

End the exercise after two or three minutes. Then discuss how the process went. Was the turn-taking smooth? Did you collaborate? Did one of you try to force any ideas? Did ideas evolve as you proceeded? How was the give-and-take of collaboration during that process? Discuss the process for each of you, and moments of interest to you. What lessons might you take from this activity in relation to your co-working? What have you learned about yourselves?

If you would like another go, you can try drawing other objects together. Or, you can go freestyle and begin the process not knowing what you will create. Interesting creations may result!

Questions to consider:

- What is your understanding of the reasons for establishing common ground with new colleagues?
- What is the difference between a basic assumption group and a working group?
- What reflections do you have about the discussion topics? Have you discussed any of these topics with a colleague? How did it go? What are you learning about yourself and your colleague(s)? How can this benefit the work you do together and how you support each other and help each other develop as professionals?
- Have you used the worksheets? How can you incorporate those into your co-working processes and supervision?

Worksheet 1: Our co-working agreement

(adapt and use as needed)

Names . . . .

Date . . . .

Location . . . .

. . . .

Supervisor/Mentor/Manager . . . .

We have discussed the following topic areas:

. . . .

. . . .

. . . .

. . . .

. . . .

Areas of agreement/common goals:

. . . .

. . . .

. . . .

. . . .

. . . .

Areas for further discussion:

. . . .

. . . .

. . . .

. . . .

. . . .

Areas where we need supervision, support or mentoring:

. . . .

. . . .

. . . .

. . . .

. . . .

Copyright © Clark Baim 2014

Our next supervision/mentoring session is with . . . .

. . . .

on (date and time) . . . .

Signatures and date

. . . .

. . . .

Copyright © Clark Baim 2014

✔

Worksheet 2: Am I ready to be a co-worker?

(adapt and use as needed)

Use this worksheet to gauge how ready you are to be a mindful co-worker and a collaborative colleague.

In my opinion, what are the pros and cons of co-working?

. . . .

. . . .

. . . .

What do I value in myself that I would like my co-worker to know about?

. . . .

. . . .

. . . .

What do I value about them that I would like them to know about?

. . . .

. . . .

. . . .

What do I want to achieve from having a co-worker? How will I periodically check that this is happening?

. . . .

. . . .

. . . .

What would I find difficult to talk about with my co-worker?

. . . .

. . . .

. . . .

Self-rating: 1 is low, 5 is high

Do I really value the contributions of my co-workers?	1 2 3 4 5
How flexible am I, for example flexible about incorporating new learning or different co-working styles?	1 2 3 4 5
How accurate is my self-reflection on my work and on my co-working?	1 2 3 4 5
How well do I receive constructive critical feedback?	1 2 3 4 5

Copyright © Clark Baim 2014

How pro-active am I about seeking feedback about ways to improve my working practices and skills? 1 2 3 4 5

How well do I actually reflect on feedback and change my practice as a result? (What is my evidence for this?) 1 2 3 4 5

To what extent do I look to my colleagues for feedback and examples of good practice? 1 2 3 4 5

Am I prepared to let the other person shine, progress, etc.? (What are my genuine hopes for them?) 1 2 3 4 5

How able am I to channel my competitive feelings in constructive ways? 1 2 3 4 5

Do I really want to share leadership, or collaborate? 1 2 3 4 5

How able am I to work to the five principles of mindful co-working? (Chapter 1) 1 2 3 4 5

How able am I to practise the ten key skills of mindful co-working? (Chapter 2) 1 2 3 4 5

After answering these questions, consider whether you are ready to co-work and also whether you have any areas for development prior to co-working. A suggestion: You may wish to review your answers with your supervisor, manager or mentor, especially if there are any areas for development.

Copyright © Clark Baim 2014

CHAPTER 4
Planning Together

In this chapter you will learn:
- how to structure planning sessions so that they enhance the effectiveness of your work
- how proper attention to planning sessions and other work can contribute to professional development.

Mindful co-working is like a muscle: to keep it toned and in shape you have to work at it. Lack of attention can make the co-working relationship lose strength or go rigid. And who wants a floppy co-working relationship? So we need regular processes for keeping the co-working relationship in tip-top shape. Careful and deliberate planning is one of these key processes.

Mindful planning should include a consideration of the aims and content of the work to be done, and also of the processes that you will use to undertake the work. In situations where co-workers are leading groups or presentations, planning also includes discussion of which worker will take the lead on which part of the session, how you will work together and what your shared understanding is of the aims and objectives of your tasks.

When you plan your work together with colleagues, this is also a valuable opportunity to anticipate how to help each other to develop professional skills and confidence. For example, we can share with our co-worker the areas we are trying to develop, and ask for feedback afterwards. Similarly, we can ask our colleagues what areas they are trying to develop, and offer them feedback in a way that they feel they can appreciate and benefit from.

Below you will find some general points of guidance for you and your co-workers to use in planning your work together. Use the topics below as a point of reference, including items that are relevant to your work. At the end of the chapter there is a worksheet template that you can use for planning sessions.

THE CHECK-IN

When you begin your planning session, try starting with a check-in with your colleagues. You might start with a few simple but important questions:

- What thoughts and feelings am I bringing to the session, or to the work, today? How am I within myself?

- Do I need to leave anything 'outside the door' in order to focus my energies on the task?

- After discussing the first two items, agree your agenda for the planning session.

CONSIDER THE AIMS AND CONTENT OF THE SESSION OR PIECE OF WORK YOU WILL UNDERTAKE TOGETHER

What are the aims and expected outcomes of this piece of work? What are the benchmarks for success, and what methods will we use to measure progress? What content will we include and in what sequence? How will we structure the session?

REVIEW PRIOR KNOWLEDGE AND CONTEXT FOR THE WORK

Next, review any prior knowledge of the person, group or organization you will be working with. Bring yourselves up to date with what has been happening recently and where your work will fit into the bigger picture.

PRACTICAL MATTERS

Anticipate how to use the room. Where will people and visual aids be positioned? Are there any health and safety issues (for example, if we will be using technical equipment or if people will be active during sessions). Are there safety issues in the building or in relation to security that we need to take into account?

SPECIAL NEEDS

Do any of us have special needs? How can this be taken into account in our planning? Similarly, do any of our participants/clients have special needs? How can we take this into account in our planning?

CONSIDER POSSIBLE BLOCKS TO SUCCESS AND STRATEGIES TO WORK AROUND THEM

Anticipate issues or problems that may arise. What obstacles might there be in the work we are about to do together? What strengths and weaknesses might there be in the person, group or organization we are working with, and how can we take these into account in our planning?

Where relevant: Discuss the anticipated group dynamics and what approach we will be taking with individuals in the group. What strategies will we use if there is confrontation or disruption from within the group?

CULTURAL DIFFERENCE AND ANTI-DISCRIMINATORY PRACTICE

What cultural issues and anti-discriminatory practice issues do we need to take into account when undertaking this session or piece of work? How will this affect our co-working and also our interactions with the client(s), audience, customers? For example, are there cultural assumptions that we need to check out and clarify, or are there any prejudices we may need to become more aware of, in order to minimize the possibility of discriminatory practice?

RECORDING PLANNING AND DE-BRIEF SESSIONS

Planning for recording what took place in a session or at work generally may be time consuming, but it pays dividends later on.

I have on occasion videoed planning and de-brief sessions with my colleagues. This has a powerful effect of focusing the mind on the task. It also provides useful learning opportunities. For example, if our work during a session does not go well, or if our co-working goes astray, often this could be pre-empted by better planning and preparation.

For supervisors and managers, asking your supervisees to record their planning and de-brief sessions may seem a little too much like 'Big Brother'. However, if you explain your reasons and gain consent, it can be an enriching experience for all. It must be done in the spirit of mutual trust and professional development, and never with a sense of being spied on and never in a clandestine manner.

CONSIDER YOUR OWN AREAS OF DEVELOPMENT

In your planning sessions, we suggest you review with each other the professional skills you are working on. Each co-worker should take some responsibility for helping their co-worker to address issues of professional development, and to give them feedback at the end of the session.

As part of this process, you can ask each other, 'How will I know if you are experiencing that difficulty…?' Then you can plan how you will support and assist each other during the session. For example, if co-worker X is trying to work on his ability to keep to the structure and aims of a piece of work, it might be that co-worker Y can assist by asking questions and making suggestions that will help co-worker X to keep himself on task.

Not only can we share with our colleague the areas we are trying to develop, we can also ask for feedback. Similarly, we can ask our colleagues what areas they are trying to develop, and offer them feedback in a way that they feel they can appreciate and benefit from.

If you use this strategy, it is crucial to plan ahead. *There is a delicate balance between being helpful and being annoying and controlling.*

By planning ahead, each worker will know why the other is asking such prompting questions.

DIVIDE AND DELEGATE TASKS

At this stage of the planning session, the co-workers divide up what roles each worker will have during the session or piece of work. Which exercises will need a *lead worker/co-worker* format and which will use *shared co-working* (see Chapter 2)? Who will take responsibility for recording work, where relevant? Who will introduce the topic?

Consider the broader agency context of your working together. For example, is there a staff development agenda, where a senior staff member is intended to help develop a newer staff member?

GIVING PLANNING ENOUGH TIME

How long is enough time for planning? This will depend on the context and the nature of the task. Situations where more time is needed for planning include: if it is the first time co-workers are running a session together; if the task is complex; if co-workers have only recently begun working together; if there are broader organizational issues or issues to do with the people you will be working with or presenting to that need to be discussed; or if a co-worker expresses the need for more planning due to particular issues, personal or professional.

WHO NEEDS TO BE THERE FOR THE PLANNING?

All co-workers should be present for the full planning session(s), and they should be on time. It is also important that colleagues clear the diary for these planning sessions, so they can focus on the task in hand. It is one of those certainties in life that if a colleague consistently comes late to planning sessions, is distracted during planning sessions, or otherwise undermines the planning, there will be steady erosion in co-working, performance and morale. If you are late or constantly checking the phone during planning sessions, be aware of the effect this has on your co-workers. If you are all doing it, that's not planning, it's communal electronic grazing.

COMPLETE YOUR PLANNING BEFORE
THE SESSION BEGINS

Finally, at the risk of stating the obvious, complete your planning and setup on time. This will allow you to be relaxed and ready to welcome your participants, clients, customers or audience as they arrive or as the session begins.

Questions to consider:
- What is your understanding about how to structure planning sessions so that they enhance the effectiveness of your work?
- How can proper planning contribute to professional development?
- How do planning sessions currently take place in your work setting? Any changes needed?
- What elements of this chapter apply to your workplace?
- What adaptations would you need to make?

✓

Worksheet 3: Planning record

(Adapt and use as needed. This worksheet is intended to help provide structure to planning sessions, to serve as a written record of your planning and also as a record of your development as co-workers. Some items might only be discussed and agreed but not written down.)

Names . . . .

. . . .

Date . . . .

Location . . . .

Supervisor/Mentor/Manager . . . .

. . . .

Session or piece of work being planned (date, time, title, etc.)

Our planning session ran from . . . . . to . . . . . on (date) . . . . .

At (location) . . . .

. . . .

Present for the planning were (names) . . . .

. . . .

(indicate if anyone mentioned was present for only part of the planning session)

We discussed the following:

1. the aims, expected outcomes and/or content of the session or piece of work (brief summary)

2. prior knowledge and context for the work (brief summary of areas discussed)

3. equipment and learning aids needed (specify)

4. are there any potential or likely difficulties we anticipate, for example with the group dynamic, individuals in the group, technical issues and anything else that we can plan for?

5. issues of cultural difference and anti-discriminatory practice, and our plan of action to take these into account

6. possible blocks to success and strategies to work around them

7. how will we record/write up our session/document our work?

8. our own areas of development (indicate areas of development that each person is working on, and the agreed processes for helping each other before, during and after the session)

Copyright © Clark Baim 2014

9. divide and delegate tasks (Who will do which tasks? How will we hand over and share leadership during the session?)

10. what are our mutual expectations of each other?

11. areas we would like feedback on from our supervisor/mentor/manager (include areas where further guidance or training are needed).

Notes . . . .

. . . .

. . . .

Signed and dated by all present . . . .

. . . .

. . . .

Copyright © Clark Baim 2014

CHAPTER 5
De-briefing

In this chapter, you will learn:

- the importance of full de-briefing in mindful co-working
- how to give and receive positive and constructive critical feedback
- ten points to bear in mind about feedback
- 'I'm OK – you're OK' communication
- a suggested structure for de-brief sessions.

At the end of any type of work delivered with colleagues, the de-briefing session provides an important opportunity to reflect on the content, process and outcomes of the work and improve performance. The de-brief also offers a crucial opportunity for colleagues to help each other to develop their skills and improve the interpersonal dynamics of their professional relationship to make the outcomes of their work even more effective.

Where de-briefing is done thoroughly and with integrity, it will enhance the effectiveness and efficiency of work delivered. An added benefit is that good co-working has a positive effect on team dynamics; team members who observe effective co-working want to be part of the action – particularly when they see that excellent co-working gets positive results.

Conversely, where de-briefing is ignored or done in a haphazard way (going through the motions) it is, at the least, a lost opportunity, but more commonly will lead to under-performance and adversely affect the quality of work over time.

During de-briefing sessions, there must be free communication and trust between co-workers. You and your co-workers should be able to trust that, beyond the session, each of you will speak of the others with respect, even when there are areas of disagreement between you.

There are several important elements to effective de-briefs. The first element is *feedback*, and for the purposes of clarity we will break this concept into two headings: positive feedback and constructive critical feedback.

POSITIVE FEEDBACK

Co-workers can and should give each other positive feedback during de-briefs, and this should be specific feedback, not just along the lines of, *'Yes, I think you did a good job in that session.'*

An example of more specific positive feedback would be,

> 'Yes, I noticed that you dealt with that awkward question really well. What I noticed was that you asked the customer to explain their concerns fully, and then you summarized what they said and ensured you understood. You then offered a clear explanation which addressed their concerns and you checked to see what their response was. What I learned from that is how you can respond to situations like that and get a good outcome.'

Notice in this example how the person offering the positive feedback also noted with appreciation something they learned from their colleague. This is not always relevant, but it can be a very enriching form of positive feedback when we appreciate each others' skills in this way.

Interestingly, some people find it very difficult to give and receive positive feedback. They seem to rush to the negative. If you or your co-worker find it difficult to receive or give positive feedback, this is something that needs to be addressed in discussion and planning, because it could prove to be an obstacle to effective de-briefing. One colleague I recall would constantly bat away any positive feedback, in effect saying, 'No I was awful' to anything I offered. That wasn't helpful, actually, and it put me in the position where I constantly had to make extra effort to reassure her and support her. Not fun.

Just as a little pointer, you can use this simple structure for positive feedback: 'One thing I really liked about what you did was…because…'

CONSTRUCTIVE CRITICAL FEEDBACK

Colleagues have often told me that offering and receiving constructive critical feedback is the most difficult and anxiety-inducing aspect of their professional life. Nevertheless, if constructive critical feedback is done with sensitivity, integrity, respect and good will (i.e. if delivered using emotional intelligence), it can greatly enhance working relationships and lead to better performance outcomes within individuals and teams.

Constructive critical feedback must be given calmly and clearly, without being affected by the heat of emotion which can sometimes cloud communication and lead to hurt feelings. Remember that it is the issue or the behaviour that is being addressed, not the person.

When offering constructive critical feedback, the person giving the feedback must take a positive approach and give *specific evidence* to their colleague and not simply 'dump feelings' or make sweeping statements. This may mean coming back to the issue at a later time, after feelings have had time to settle and after the person giving the feedback has had time to consider fully the most respectful and productive way forward. The person giving feedback must also take responsibility for first identifying whether or not they have any unresolved issues (e.g. unresolved feelings about previous co-workers; competitive feelings; feelings about the work itself; old patterns of response being triggered, including patterns started early in life) that may influence their ability to see the issue clearly and logically.

The person receiving the difficult feedback also has a part to play: they must listen with an open mind and be willing to engage in constructive discussion and honest, realistic self-critique without becoming emotionally defensive, rigid, distraught, angry or taking the victim role. Otherwise, the co-workers will be unable to work honestly and constructively with each other.

Here is an example of constructive critical feedback, and a mindful response (we must assume that the two workers have a good foundation of rapport and trust for this feedback to occur):

Carmen: What I experienced today was you talking over several of my points. For example, when I was talking about the projected budget, which was the part I was meant to deliver, you re-stated the same point I had just made on several occasions. That left me feeling confused, because I thought we had agreed that I would deliver that part. I think it diminished my role from the point of view of the customers. Can you explain how you saw that situation?

Daniel: Yes, I know what you're referring to. I spoke out of turn, and I apologize. I think it was because I was so anxious that they accepted the budget. It doesn't have anything to do with my trust in your ability; it's more about how I manage my anxiety and my determination to win contracts. I'm glad you pointed this out to me, because I think these sorts of interactions are unhelpful and I think customers often get a sense that something is wrong when we don't seem to be on the same wavelength. Next time I will keep to plan.

OTHER POINTS TO CONSIDER ABOUT FEEDBACK

1. Feedback should address the work as a whole and also consider how the co-working relationship affected the outcome of the task undertaken.

2. Both co-workers should take responsibility for giving and receiving feedback in a clear, unambiguous format that enhances, without diminishing, the co-working relationship.

3. Feedback should be focused on finding a solution to enhance each person's learning and contribution as a professional.

4. Feedback that implies changes are needed should be specific, achievable and realistic. Colleagues should join together to make improvements. Where changes are called for, the underlying question should always be, 'How can we work together to make things better?'

5. Feedback should be offered in an emotionally smooth manner. This means we don't dump our emotions on our

colleagues. Each worker has responsibility to contain hot emotions until they have had time to process them, reflect on them, and decide the best way to communicate about the difficulties with their co-worker. Feedback delivered in anger or in a frustrated tone will usually create anger in return, or fear, resentment and sometimes – as we saw in the introduction to this book – fist fights. At the very least, it contributes to an unhappy work environment.

6. All feedback should be treated as a gift, and delivered with respect and care. It should be based on a fundamental respect for your colleague as a human being.

7. Feedback says as much about the giver as the receiver.

8. A good option, if available, is to have a third party lead the de-brief. This can be helpful in many circumstances, especially in situations where the co-workers have to deal with very complex situations where emotions are running high. In such instances, an external facilitator can help the co-workers to sort through their complex work and reflect on their emotions.

9. A very useful technique to try before offering someone feedback is first to ask, '*How do you like your feedback?*' This invites the person receiving the feedback to be an active recipient rather than a passive listener. It is the sort of question that can add dynamism and maturity to the de-briefing conversation.

10. When giving and receiving feedback, it is very important to remember and put into practice our best skills in active listening and emotionally and socially intelligent communication.

THE OK CORRAL

In Chapter 1, brief mention was made of Transactional Analysis and Eric Berne in reference to the concept of adult-adult communication. Another useful concept from Transactional Analysis sometimes goes by the name the 'OK Corral'.[1] The 'OK Corral' offers a short-hand way of understanding human interaction in terms of people's concept of themselves and others. It goes like this:

I'm OK – you're OK: This is win-win interaction. It represents mature, adult and emotionally intelligent communication among colleagues.

I'm not OK – you're OK: This stance forces your co-worker to rescue you or puts them in the position of the oppressor.

I'm OK – you're not OK: This approach turns you into the oppressor and will drive away your colleagues over time.

I'm not OK – you're not OK: This attitude drives you both apart and probably tends toward burn-out for you and/or your colleague.

In order for de-brief to work well, co-workers need to follow the principle of 'I'm OK – you're OK' communication in the de-brief session.

STRUCTURE FOR DE-BRIEFING

As a general rule, de-briefing should include a discussion about three key areas: Content, Process and Personal Reflections.

Content

In this part of the de-briefing, co-workers review the *content* of the session. Questions can include:

- Did we achieve the aims we set out to?
- How well prepared were we to deliver the session? Did we know our material?
- Did we keep to our plan, or adjust it appropriately in response to contingencies or to the needs of the participants/clients/customers?
- If yes, how did we achieve that?

---

1   Ernst, F. (2008) *Transactional Analysis in the OK Corral: Grid for What's Happening.* Vallejo, CA: Addresso' Set Publications. Available at http://franklinernst.com/OK_Corral. html, accessed on 27 September 2013.

- If not, why not? How can we improve next time?
- What went well?
- What went not so well?
- How well did we meet the requirements of the agency/ organization/context in which we work?

Process

Here, co-workers discuss and review the *process* of the session. Topics include both the *overt* and *covert* processes.

Overt processes

By this is meant the processes that are obvious and visible. Questions that will help to address overt processes include:

- What did I do well?
- What would I do differently?
- How was our co-working? Did we keep to agreed principles of co-working? If yes, how did we do that? If not, why not? And how can we improve for next time?
- What was happening between us as workers and the people we were working with/presenting to?
- To what extent were we professional, thorough, approachable and open?
- How did we respond to questions? How was our questioning and listening?
- Something I really liked about your work…
- How was our praise and reinforcement? Did we encourage the people with whom we were working?
- Did we encourage participation and the sharing of ideas and expertise?

Let's rate our interpersonal process as co-workers on a scale of one to ten (see Chapter 1 for the rating scale). Do we agree on the rating? If not, let's explore the different perceptions. If we do agree, what's behind our rating? Why did we give ourselves that rating? Is it justified by the evidence?

More advanced and challenging: Let's rate ourselves in terms of the level of mindfulness in our communication (see Appendix I for the rating scale). Let's each score each other and ourselves. How do the scores compare? Where do we agree or differ? What's behind the differences? What evidence are we drawing upon to make our assessments? Who could offer us objective feedback? How can we explore these differences and come out stronger?

Covert processes

When considering process issues, it can be useful to look at the *covert* processes in the session:

- Was there any subtext in our interactions with each other – verbal or non-verbal – that we need to discuss? What did we do well? How can we improve next time?

- How equal or unequal is our co-working relationship during planning, co-working and de-briefing?

- Was there any subtext among or between the people we worked with? Who interacted with whom, who interrupted when and why, who avoided eye contact with whom? How did we manage this? Is there anything we need to do to address this next time?

- Was there any subtext in our interactions with our participants/clients/customers? Did we get caught out by any interactions that we might have handled better? How did we handle any pressing or contentious issues that might have arisen?

- Were there any external factors that impacted on the session? For example, how well is the organization or agency supporting this work? How well organized was the session? How well thought out is the physical environment in which we are working, and how well supported are the staff with whom we work? How can we help to improve these and other external factors? What role do we have in this?

PERSONAL REFLECTIONS

In this part of the de-briefing, co-workers share their personal reflections on the session. This can include reflections on our thoughts and feelings about our performance in relation to the session, to each other as workers, and to the people with whom we work. Questions can include:

- What feelings am I left with after the session? What feelings do I have about the content of the session, the process, or any other issues arising from the session?

- How do I feel about my performance in the session?

- What did I do well?

- What can I do differently next time?

- What was helpful about the day?

- What wasn't?

- What should have happened?

- Was I clear about what I was meant to be doing?

- Did I properly anticipate problems?

- How did I deal with anticipated and unanticipated problems? What did I learn? What would I do differently next time? How can I improve my skills as a co-worker? What help do I need? Where can I get it?

- How did we support each other and work together?

- How able did I feel to talk with my co-worker about difficulties? If I could not, what got in the way? Were these my blocks or my co-worker's? What responsibility do I have? How and when am I going to raise this with my co-worker and/or supervisor?

- How did I improve against my targets for learning and professional development? Did I meet any personal obstacles? How can I improve next time? How can I involve my co-worker in this process (if appropriate)?

ISSUES TO ADDRESS OUTSIDE OF THE DE-BRIEFING SESSION

In this part of the de-briefing, co-workers may choose to note – in general terms only – any issues that they feel will be best addressed out of the workplace, for example with mentors, with line managers or in personal counselling. The co-worker should respect this and not probe for further details. Some issues affecting co-workers are better first discussed outside of the co-working relationship – for example in confidential counselling or with a line manager – and might never be discussed between the co-workers. These may include:

- personal impact issues of the work
- sexual attraction to one's co-worker or from one's co-worker
- sexual attraction to a client
- negative feelings (or transferences) towards your co-worker and/or clients
- unresolved trauma or loss
- the impact of working with a colleague who is personally or professionally stuck, depressed, burnt out, excessively competitive or seemingly on a professional 'mission'
- the impact of working with a colleague whose performance or ethos conflicts with the aims and objectives of the organization or agency
- grievance, disciplinary matters and professional incompetence.

INVITATION TO A STANDING OVATION

An important role that co-workers can have in relation to each other is the role of encourager. With this in mind, perhaps we might think of the de-brief session as a time for offering each other a metaphorical standing ovation on a regular basis. Life is short – let's encourage and appreciate each other while we're here. (You could even drop the idea that it's a metaphor and make it an actual standing ovation.) Why not applaud and tell your co-worker you think they're great at something? You may be amazed at how people become more confident and develop when they have an enthusiastic co-worker who champions their development.

Questions to consider:

- What is your understanding of the different purposes of de-briefing?

- What are your thoughts about the best ways to give and receive positive and constructive critical feedback?

- Can you describe 'I'm OK – you're OK' communication and the 'OK Corral?'

- In the suggested structure for de-briefs, what is your understanding of the purpose of including discussion of content, process and personal reflections? What are three or four topics that are more suited to supervision, which you might not ever raise with your co-worker?

- How can you incorporate the topics on Worksheet 4 into your practice as a co-worker?

Worksheet 4: De-briefing agreement

(adapt and use as needed)

We have agreed to the following principles in giving and receiving positive and constructive critical feedback. We agree to these principles in the understanding that open, honest and confidential feedback is a key to our effectiveness as colleagues and our professional development.

Date . . . .

Location . . . .

Supervisor/mentor/manager . . . .

. . . .

My name and role . . . .

. . . .

What I will and will not do when…

Giving positive and constructive critical feedback to . . . .

. . . .

Receiving feedback from . . . .

Areas of development I am working on:

Professional skills and knowledge . . . .

. . . .

Interpersonal skills and interactions . . . .

. . . .

Self-awareness and self-regulation skills . . . .

. . . .

What do we need to bring to supervision? . . . .

. . . .

My name and role . . . .

. . . .

What I will and will not do when…

Giving positive and constructive critical feedback to . . . .

. . . .

Receiving feedback from . . . .

. . . .

Copyright © Clark Baim 2014

✓

Areas of development I am working on:

Professional skills and knowledge . . . .

. . . .

Interpersonal skills and interactions . . . .

. . . .

Self-awareness and self-regulation skills . . . .

. . . .

What do we need to bring to supervision?

Notes:. . . . .

. . . .

. . . .

Signatures and date . . . .

. . . .

. . . .

Copyright © Clark Baim 2014

CHAPTER 6

Supervision for Co-workers

In this chapter, you will learn:

- the definition of supervision
- the four functions of supervision
- the reflective practice model
- questions based on the reflective practice model
- the importance of being a mindful supervisor
- four tools for supervision.

In this chapter, we consider how the supervisor can help colleagues develop mindful co-working skills, including the skills of working through difficulties when they inevitably arise.

Depending on the type of organization you work for, supervision may take a number of different forms. Sometimes it comes in the form of line management, and in other situations it may come in the form of case supervision, clinical supervision, mentoring, coaching, clinical de-briefing or consultation. In some organizations, people have more than one type of supervision. For example, in some health and social care settings, where staff are dealing with highly complex and emotionally challenging cases, professionals have line management supervision with their manager and clinical supervision with a therapeutically trained supervisor or external counsellor. Whatever form of supervision you have, if you work in close collaboration with colleagues, part of the supervision should include a consideration of the co-working process itself.

DEFINING SUPERVISION

What is meant by the term *supervision*?

> Supervision is a process by which one worker is given responsibility by the organisation to work with another worker(s) in order to meet certain organisational, professional and personal objectives which together promote the best outcomes for service users. (Morrison 2005, p.32[1])

This definition, with some adaptation, can be applied to supervision in most organizations. Supervision helps workers to be clear about their purpose and tasks, and also helps workers to reflect on the emotional dimensions and meaning of their work. Supervision offers a regular, containing opportunity for workers to reflect on what is going on for their clients, and also for themselves. The supervisory relationship should be one where achievements are celebrated and built upon, and challenges are explored. The supervisor can support workers as they critically evaluate their work. This can be a rewarding and challenging role for supervisors.[2]

Supervisors who provide supervision to pairs, groups or teams of workers can bring a broader awareness of the systems around the co-working unit. This is a crucial factor not only in helping the co-workers to understand the importance and role they serve in the wider functioning of the organization, but it can also help co-workers to understand how their functioning as co-workers can impact on the wider system.

THE FOUR FUNCTIONS OF SUPERVISION

No matter what our occupational title is, if our work involves understanding and helping people, we need a combination of four things from our supervisor. These four functions of supervision may come together in one relationship, or they may be allocated to different relationships within and outside the workplace. According to Morrison, the four broad functions of supervision are:[3]

---

1   Morrison, T. (2005) *Staff Supervision in Social Care.* Brighton: Pavilion Publishers.

2   Ruch, G., Turney, D. and Ward, A. (2010) *Relationship-based Social Work: Getting to the Heart of Practice.* London: Jessica Kingsley Publishers.

3   Morrison, T. (2005) *Staff Supervision in Social Care.* Brighton: Pavilion Publishers.

1. *The managerial function:* To help workers assess how well they are fulfilling their roles. This function includes a focus on management, accountability and quality assurance.

2. *The support function:* To support workers and ensure their well-being, including reflecting on the emotional impact of their work.

3. *The professional development function:* To develop workers and broaden their skills and knowledge. This function of supervision is also focused on helping workers to develop their ability to reflect on their work and to learn and adapt to new situations.

4. *The mediation function:* To clarify roles, mediate between workers, obtain and allocate resources, and deal with complaints. Supervisors who carry out this function help workers to negotiate their relationships with other workers and with the organization.

To some extent, co-workers can carry out some of these functions themselves in their planning and de-brief sessions. For example, co-workers can help each other to *develop* and they can also lend *support* to one another on a daily basis where needed. Supervision is not the exclusive domain of the 'expert' and it is not a process that should be hidden behind mists of arcane wisdom. Supervision can be undertaken among co-workers, peer groups and peer networks, as well as with an officially designated supervisor. Looked at in this way, supervision should be seen as an everyday activity performed at the grass roots – something that workers can do to help themselves immediately, with or without the help of an officially designated supervisor.

Yet there are some functions that are only appropriately carried out by someone who is designated with the authority and responsibility of the supervisor or manager. The functions that are more clearly the domain of the supervisor are the managerial function and the mediation function. These functions are not exclusive to the role of the supervisor, but a number of the tasks within these domains are appropriate only to a supervisor – for example, handling formal complaints or negotiating for resources with other parts of the organization.

A supervisor is also well placed to identify tension, collusion or confusion between and among co-workers.

THE REFLECTIVE PRACTICE MODEL

When a supervisor is helping co-workers to think about their experiences and processes with each other, it may be useful to have a model for encouraging reflection and learning. One of the best known models for encouraging reflective practice is David Kolb's Experiential Learning Model,[4] sometimes also called the Reflective Practice Cycle. It is composed of four elements:

- *Focus on experience:* That is, the factual details of an experience, as complete as possible.

- *Focus on reflection:* This includes the workers' feelings and any links with previous experiences and patterns of response. It also includes helping workers to make links with their skills and knowledge.

- *Focus on analysis and meaning:* This includes probing for meaning and understanding of the situation from different perspectives, and using relevant theory as required. It also includes identifying what is unknown and in need of further discussion or reflection.

- *Focus on action plans and testing new ideas:* Here the focus is on translating the previous reflections into plans, preparation and action. It also includes setting target and criteria for success, and formulating contingency plans.

The four-step process is repeated continually as part of an ongoing learning process. The model is a simple but powerful tool, often used in education, business, social care and many other professions to encourage reflective practice. The four elements form a cycle that can begin anywhere but usually starts with a focus on recalling the details of an experience. With co-workers, this could, for example, be an account of a session they have recently conducted together.

---

4   Kolb, D. (1988) 'The process of experiential learning.' In D. Kolb (ed.) *Experience as the Source of Learning and Development.* London: Prentice Hall.

Questions based on the Reflective Practice Cycle

As a supervisor, you can use this model to help you structure your thinking about the right questions to ask your supervisees. This can be particularly useful when co-workers are experiencing difficulties, for example if one or more of them seems stuck, or if they are experiencing difficulties in their co-working relationship. Here are some ideas to get you started. It is not intended that supervisors should use all of these questions; use only the questions that are needed, and adapt them to suit the context and purpose of your supervision.[5]

Questions focused on recalling the experience

- What was the aim of the session or piece of work?
- What happened before the event? What planning had you and your co-worker(s) done?
- What happened? Describe the event with as much detail as you can recall.
- What did you say and do? What methods did you use?
- What moments particularly stand out for you? Did anything puzzle or surprise you?
- What went smoothly and to plan? What didn't?
- If your colleague(s) or the customer/client/participant told about this event from their point of view, how would they describe it?
- If you were to describe this interaction in TA (transactional analysis) terms (parent/adult/child), would you say that you and your colleagues were in adult-to-adult communication, or some other?
- Similarly, if you were to describe your interactions in terms of the Drama Triangle (victim/persecutor/rescuer), what would you say?
- What choices did you make during the session or piece of work? What changes did you make as you went along?
- What did you say or do after the session?

---

5   Adapted from Morrison, T. (2003) *Staff Supervision in Social Care*. Brighton: Pavilion Publishers.

- How are you feeling now about that experience? How has it affected you? How has it affected your sense of progress as a worker, and your hopes and aspirations in the work?

- Has anything been triggered in you that has happened before or which reminds you of something that happened before? How was this managed before, by you and by your supervisors/organization?

- What training and developmental needs does this episode highlight for you?

Questions focused on reflection

- Describe the feelings you experienced during the session or event. Describe how your feelings changed during the episode.

- What ideas did you have during that episode?

- What feelings might have been suppressed or unacknowledged during the episode that you can reflect on and name now?

- How did your feelings affect your behaviour in the session? Is this a familiar pattern? Where have you experienced anything similar in terms of your emotional reaction to situations? Give examples.

- In order for me to respond most helpfully, tell me what happens when you feel confused, distressed, scared or angry. What would you notice in each other? In yourself? What would I notice as a supervisor that would alert me to this? Now let's explore some of the underlying meaning of those responses, and maybe we can develop a plan for preventing, minimizing or working with those strategies.

- What do you think the client/customer/patient was feeling during that episode? What feelings of theirs might you have been carrying (i.e. what transference or projection processes may have been going on)?

- What feelings do you have now about the episode?

- Has anything been left unsaid or unfinished between you and your co-worker(s) or between you and the client(s), customer(s), etc.?
- Let's explore together whether there is anything unhelpful or disempowering in your patterns of response to this situation. For example, let's think about any thoughts or feelings you had when the situation became heated, or sad, or scary.
- Let's look together at some similar situations you have faced in the past, and how you responded in those situations.

Questions focused on analysis and meaning

- How would you explain what happened in that situation? What theoretical models can help us to understand what was happening between you and your colleague(s) and/or you and the client(s)?
- What went well, or not so well? Tell me about a golden moment in your work together. Do you both/all agree it was a golden moment? What made it a golden moment for you? What does it tell you about your abilities and competence in the role?
- How typical or atypical was the process that occurred in this episode?
- What were you happy about in this session? What did you do well?
- What would you do differently?
- What aims were and were not achieved?
- How clear were you about what your co-worker(s) wanted from you or were expecting you to do? Did your priorities and theirs match?
- What does this session reveal about your strengths and areas for development as a worker?
- To what extent was this episode influenced by factors such as gender, age, seniority, race, culture, etc.?

- What conclusions do you have about this situation so far, in particular your role in the situation? How do you apportion responsibility for this episode to you and your colleagues? What portion of responsibility is yours? Your colleague's? The client's?

- Did you learn anything about each other in this session? And, similarly, did you learn anything new about the client? What new information emerged? What was the key moment when this happened? How do you want to use this to improve things in the future?

- What fears or concerns do you have about doing this task? Are any of these related to gender, race, age or cultural issues, or any related issues?

- How well do the theoretical and political perspectives you hold match our agency's policies, ethical and legal obligations? Are there any possible contradictions? How will you adjust to meet the organizational requirements?

- Is there any need to go back to basics with the co-working relationship? For example, do you need, as co-workers, to discuss the common ground questions in Chapter 3? Or re-visit principles or skills of co-working in Chapters 1 and 2?

Questions focused on action plans and testing new ideas

- What needs to be done next? Does anything need urgent follow-up?

- What is working well, that you would like to keep doing?

- What would success look like when you work together again?

- What is the most important thing the clients/customers/patients need from you as a co-working team? What would be a successful outcome from their perspective?

- What areas of discomfort do you need to stick with and work through together with your colleagues – because these issues are important?

- What patterns of response do you *not* want to repeat?

- What support would help you? Who else needs to be involved? What would you need from them?
- What information do you need before proceeding?
- What help can I give as a supervisor?
- Are there any safety issues we need to be mindful of before you go forth? How can we minimize and manage risk?
- What is optional and what is non-negotiable in this situation?
- How can we ensure that you attend every supervision session? (Ask this if attendance is an issue.)
- How able are you adequately to plan for and prepare your work together? What might be getting in the way? How can we work together to ensure that your workload is balanced so that you can use your skills productively?
- Are there any training needs that need to be addressed?

BEING A MINDFUL SUPERVISOR

If you want mindful co-working to permeate your organization, it is important that all of the managers and supervisors also perform their role mindfully. If they don't, the mindful approach will go only skin deep. It will become an act, and workers will be forced to conform cynically to behavioural standards that feel imposed and contrived. Consider the contrast between these two interactions between a supervisor and a member of staff:

> 'Susan, this needs to be better. It's your job to fix it.' (Walks away.)

> 'Susan, how can we work together to make this better today?' (Pauses, listens.)

The first statement may assert the supervisor's authority and make them feel powerful and in command. Susan may do her job, but will be motivated by fear or appeasing her angry supervisor. She will probably also resent the tone of the instruction and grow distrustful of her supervisor. Hate and dread are not the best motivating feelings.

The second intervention, given in the form of a question, indicates that the supervisor considers herself to be a part of the inter-dependent network of collaborators in the organization, all working to a common goal. It's also a solution-focused question, and refers to taking immediate action today, not at an unknown future time. This is the difference between mindful supervision and mindless, hierarchical approaches to employee management. The structure of the question, and the message it conveys about shared responsibility and mutual endeavour, has been shown to have a profound effect in organizations. This seemingly simple question – 'How can we work together to make this better today?'[6] – can have transformative effects on the tenor of communication across entire organizations.

SOME TOOLS FOR SUPERVISION
Levels of communication

In order to help facilitate deeper communication, trust and respect among co-workers, it can be useful to take some time in supervision to consider the levels of communication.[7] Workers are often intrigued by this model, and I have seen many co-working pairs and teams eagerly take up this concept and use it to assess and enrich their levels of communication. The levels can be divided into:

- *Small Talk*: This is the most superficial level of communication, and helps us decide whether we want to get to know someone better. An example of small talk might be discussing the weather when we meet someone for the first time.

- *Facts and Information*: This is a very common form of communication in the workplace, typically used when colleagues need to discuss information in order to carry out their tasks. An example would be a team discussing a rota for staffing.

6   I am grateful to John Raddall of Quanta Consulting for this example (personal communication).

7   Ringer, T.M. and Gillis, H.L. (1995) 'Managing psychological depth in adventure programming.' *The Journal of Experiential Education 18*, 1, 41–51.

- *Ideas and Judgements:* At this level of communication, colleagues may discuss their own ideas and that of others. They may also disclose something about themselves and their personal lives.

- *Feelings and Experiences:* At this level, colleagues are able to share with each other, at some depth, their personal feelings, attitudes and experiences. Co-workers share this with each other in the expectation of tolerance, support and honest feedback.

- *Close rapport:* This is the level of greatest intellectual and emotional closeness between people. There are occasions when it is appropriate and useful for colleagues to engage in deep emotional connections, especially when dealing with difficult or painful issues that are relevant to everyone present. Not every occupation or organization will undertake work that requires such a depth of communication between colleagues. If your colleagues work under conditions of high stress, highly charged emotion, complexity and time pressure, such deep levels of communication can be highly beneficial for them.

The Pie Chart

Pie charts can be used in many ways. One way, for example, is to have a pair, group or team of co-workers divide up the slices into 'how much I contribute to the collaboration'. Then, 'how much I would like to contribute'. Or: 'Who is responsible for (x) in this co-working relationship?' Or: 'How is power shared in this co-working relationship?'

Using the pie chart in this way is intended to open up discussion of topics that may otherwise remain hidden under the surface. It can be useful to have co-workers complete their pie charts independently and then compare their responses.

Continuums

Like the pie chart, the continuum is a useful tool for opening up discussion between co-workers about their working practices and their functioning as a unit.

The two ends of the continuum are meant to represent opposite polarities, and the questions asked or statement made should be designed to encourage people to make a choice to place themselves at the point on the continuum that feels accurate from their point of view. Encourage people to think flexibly and not just in terms of yes/no, all or nothing.

Examples of continuum questions and statements:

- We share power equally when we are working together. (Agree/disagree.)
- We share the time equally when we are in session. (Agree/ disagree.)
- How happy am I with the way things are in our co-working relationship? (Unhappy/very happy.)
- How responsible am I for my role in the co-working dynamics? (0%–100%.)
- I can make choices about how I behave in the pair, team or group in future. (Agree/disagree.)
- I have an important role to play in this co-working relationship. (Agree/disagree.)
- What is my relationship like with my co-worker when we are in session/undertaking a task? (Laissez faire/equal partners/control freak.)
- There are some things that I would like to talk about with my co-worker(s) that I have not had time to yet. (Yes/no.)

- I would like us to speak more kindly to each other/take more time in planning/use our de-briefs better/each take more responsibility for keeping to time (Agree/disagree.)

Invent your own continuum questions, as appropriate to your context.

Structure for helping co-workers to discuss a rupture in their co-working relationship

You may find it helpful to use this three-step model for offering help to your supervisees:

1. *Listen:* This step includes using active listening and simple open questions. It does *not* involve offering suggestions or solutions.

2. *Guide:* This step includes asking questions that help to guide the co-workers to find their own solutions.

3. *Coach/instruct:* This step includes making plans and modelling and practising skills. For example, you may encourage co-workers to practise their communication skills using role play.

SHOULD ALL CO-WORKERS BE ABLE TO WORK WITH ANYONE?

The strategies and techniques in this book should make it possible for you to co-work with almost anyone, as long as they also work to the principles in this book. This does not necessarily mean that you will become best of friends – colleagueship is not the same as friendship – but it will mean that both of you can do a better job together.

There are occasions, however, when despite all best efforts on the part of co-workers and supervisors, workers may find that they cannot get along and work together. This may be, for example, because there is history between them that they simply cannot overcome. I can only think of two examples that I have seen where it was utterly impossible to see a way forward: one was where one colleague had officially filed a grievance against the other person, and the other was when one colleague had a sexual affair with the other's partner. I think most people would understand why co-working might be unrealistic in these circumstances.

In situations where a co-working relationship must end because the co-workers cannot get along, this should also be managed so that each worker is helped to process and understand the reasons, and also their responsibility for containing their feelings and not spreading ill will about the other.

Questions to consider:

- How is supervision defined and used in your organization?
- What is your understanding of the four functions of supervision? How are these functions carried out in your organization?
- What do you recall about the four elements of the Reflective Practice Model?
- What is your understanding of the reasons why it is important to be a mindful supervisor?
- How can you make use of the four tools for supervision in this chapter?
- How can you help develop within your organization a common language to describe how mindful co-working can enhance the work of supervisees and of the organization as a whole?
- How can you become actively involved in developing each worker's skills through shared use of the practice tools and concepts in this book?
- How can you become more attuned to the stories that workers share about their work, or even themselves as practitioners, and help them to become more integrated as practitioners?

CHAPTER 7

Ouch! Pitfalls to Avoid and Handy Hints when Things Go Wrong

In this chapter, you will learn:

- when the mindful approach is less relevant or likely to fail
- what to do when things go wrong in the co-working relationship
- some of the most common co-working 'what not to do's and how to deal with them
- how 'mistakes' can be re-framed as opportunities for pro-social modelling.

Even with the best of intentions, co-working can still go wrong, in little moments and on a larger scale. When this happens, it can be useful to be prepared in advance for such eventualities. This chapter offers a range of advice and tips for how to deal with ruptures in the co-working relationship.

A BRIEF CAVEAT ABOUT THE LIMITS OF MINDFUL CO-WORKING

In his book, *Office Politics*,[1] Oliver James warns us about the office psychopath, the narcissist and the Machiavel. His warning should

---

1   James, O. (2013) *Office Politics: How to Survive in a World of Lying, Backstabbing and Dirty Tricks.* London: Random House.

be well heeded; life certainly can offer up some very tricky and dangerous individuals.

By contrast, *this* book is largely devoted to co-working situations where co-workers have genuine good will and are serious about trying to get co-working right. In other situations, where a co-worker seems malign or sadistic, please don't try to use the principles of mindful co-working with such an individual; you will end up torturing yourself. The reality is that, with some people, no amount of collaborative discussion and planning will result in workable and mutual co-working. Such people are best avoided, and if you can't avoid them, you will need to develop the art of verbal self-defence, so you don't end up hurt or exploited.

SOME 'WHAT NOT TO DO'S

Let's consider some examples of when things can go wrong between co-workers. These examples have been offered by colleagues, or they are examples I have experienced or witnessed myself. As you reflect on the following examples, you might want to consider the impact of the behaviour in various combinations of workers, for example male/female combinations, different racial and cultural combinations among workers, and whether the behaviour occurs during shared co-working or lead worker/co-worker situations.

General workplace examples of 'what not to do's

- One worker ignores or dismisses their co-worker, non-verbally or verbally.

- A senior colleague vents their anger and frustration on to a less senior (and less fortunate) colleague.

- A worker gossips about their co-worker to other colleagues. The gossip is mean-spirited, and no one challenges it.

- A co-worker has a habit of cutting across colleagues, speaking when they do.

- One co-worker offers themselves as 'the expert', which forces the other to play the role of the 'assistant' or the 'learner driver'.

- One worker does not thank their co-worker when the co-worker makes a suggestion or an offer of some kind.
- One worker ignores another's feelings.
- One worker is being 'bossy' to the other, ordering them about while also complaining or being impatient.
- One worker allows another to deviate from safe practice without intervening. (In extreme circumstances, co-workers must retain the right to stop the process and take a time out, regardless of the rank or seniority of their co-worker.)

Examples of 'what not to do's that apply more specifically to group facilitation, training and making presentations

- A co-worker regularly tries to cut in and take over while their colleague leads an activity.
- In a presentation, one worker stands in front of the other, in effect blocking them from view.
- Two workers are co-leading a piece of work that requires that they interact with each other, yet they proceed in parallel, without reference to each other.
- A co-worker apologizes for contributing or asking a question of the lead worker. (There is no need to apologize or to ask permission to speak.)
- Workers struggle with each other for power, control, status or leadership.
- One worker sighs or shows non-verbal signals that express displeasure with a co-worker.
- A co-worker shares far too much personal information, to the point where the audience/group members look awkward or give feedback that they are uncomfortable about the personal information.
- A co-worker regularly runs far too long with their segments of the session, leaving you with too little time to run your part of the session.

- A co-worker undermines their own credibility by getting flustered and saying critical things about themselves during the session. As part of this, they may laugh nervously in a way that undermines their credibility and authority.

- Co-workers contradict each other in an uncontained or dismissive way that may cause confusion/splitting/lack of safety in the group.

- A co-worker in a group work session distracts people from focusing on the topic by slouching, leaning on walls or chairs, shuffling papers, scowling, smirking, or taking notes in a distracting manner.

With all of these examples, the remedy is fairly obvious: don't do that! If you are the sort of co-worker who does these things in the workplace, you might want to take this as a cue to modify your behaviour and to be more mindful in your approach to co-working. It would also be a good idea to pro-actively seek feedback from your co-worker as you modify the behaviour. They can let you know if it's actually making a difference.

If you have a co-worker who does some of these behaviours, it can be tricky to raise these issues with them, especially if they are typically defensive when they receive constructive critical feedback. Nevertheless, if their behaviour is affecting you and if it is affecting the quality of your work, you will need to raise it with your colleague. This calls for assertiveness and tact – in others words, emotional and social intelligence (see Chapter 1) – in order to raise the issue and assert its importance, while at the same time preserving the positive aspects of the relationship. Please see the section on constructive critical feedback in Chapter 5, where there is an example of a worker giving this form of feedback to her co-worker.

FOCUS ON GROUP WORK, TRAINING AND MAKING PRESENTATIONS: HOW CO-WORKERS CAN DEAL WITH DIFFICULT SITUATIONS IN GROUPS USING PRO-SOCIAL MODELLING

Difficult situations that arise in groups can also be seen as opportunities for pro-social modelling. This may seem a rather unusual proposition, yet if you take to heart this idea, you will find that even when things go very badly wrong in the group or with your co-worker, the repair can often make the relationship with the group or with your co-worker stronger than ever. If you repair an aspect of your co-working relationship in a 'live' situation in the presence of others, such as when you are co-running a session or co-training a group of professionals, the repair will also model for your clients, customers or audience a good example of how ruptures can be repaired in positive and mature ways.

SOME EXAMPLES OF PRO-SOCIAL MODELLING USED TO ADDRESS TRICKY SITUATIONS FACED BY CO-WORKERS
What to do if your co-worker takes over the exercise that you were leading

Sometimes co-workers can get their wires crossed about who is leading an exercise or one of them may forget who is leading an exercise. If you are the lead worker and your co-worker takes over, you need a clear and succinct way to wrest back control of the exercise. Here's an example:

Lead worker to co-worker: Thanks very much, Ben, that's been very useful to see how that model fits with this example. I'm aware of the time remaining in this session, and I think it's time we move on to cover (X). Can we leave the model there and let's keep the model in mind as we now look at (X).

In this example, the co-worker has been thanked for his contribution, and he has also been clearly informed by the lead worker that it is still her lead for this activity. The passage above contains within it a code phrase, which is the reference to 'the time remaining'. In this example, both co-workers would understand that when one of them refers to the time remaining, there is a degree of urgency to the request and they are making an earnest effort, from their point of view, to get the session and their co-working back on course.

Respectfully interrupting your colleague in order to intervene in an unproductive interaction

If it looks like your co-worker is getting into a sticky situation with a member of the group or the audience, you have a crucial role to play in helping them extract themselves from the situation. Here's a suggestion: say their name, stand (if it seems necessary) and offer an observation that registers something important is happening but also deflects the issue in some way, so that it is not just about the co-worker and the individual in the group. Here is an example I witnessed from a very experienced co-worker to her colleague, when the lead worker was getting locked into an unhelpful interaction with a group member about his resistance to the exercise everyone was doing:

> *Co-worker:* Adam, I can see that this is a point that both you and Colin feel very strongly about, and I am also aware that this activity actually calls for a range of options as to how people participate. I wonder if you think it might be an idea if Colin were to act as an observer, who could then feedback what he has observed after the activity? That would be an alternative to actually joining in in this round. I was wondering what you think, Adam?

In this example, the co-worker has clearly let Adam know that she sees the urgency of the situation, and she also offers a way out of the head to head that gives Adam options and also gives Colin options.

How can a co-worker support a lead worker who is giving incorrect information or making another type of significant error such as taking an exercise off course?

Again, this can be handled in a way that models pro-social interaction. In this example, Maria has given an incorrect instruction to the participant Rhys, and the co-worker decides it is serious enough to intervene:

> *Co-worker:* Maria, I wonder if I can just clarify with you. My understanding of the fourth step of this model is that we are looking at forming plans and actions. I noticed that Rhys and some of the group members were looking a little confused so I thought I would check with you. What do you think?

In this example, the lead worker Maria would understand that her co-worker has spotted a potential error. She would thank her co-worker and make the adjustment.

What to do if one worker 'goes blank'

If you go blank and can't think of anything to say, this is a moment to bring in your co-worker. You can let the group know your mind has gone blank, and if you do, just be sure that you don't get flustered and undermine your credibility. You can still stay in professional mode, and simply ask for help.

If your co-worker goes blank and by all appearances just does not know what to say, in the awkward silence you could interject a suggestion or two, giving your colleague time to readjust and make a choice. In more extreme situations, you may need to take over for a little while until your co-worker recovers their train of thought.

What to do if a co-worker makes a sexist comment or other prejudicial statement

This is a moment to get 'professionally curious'. I have seen this modelled by a very experienced colleague, in reply to a sexist statement made by a woman about men. The comment was along the lines of men not being able to 'do feelings'. The male worker intervened by getting 'professionally curious'. It sounded something like this:

Male worker: Ann-Marie, I'm just noting that very often in the group we encourage people to speak about specifics rather than generalizations, and I'm noting that there is often a view around in society that men have difficulty in getting in touch with and expressing their feelings. I'm really interested in this idea and I wonder if it might be useful to explore that just a little further, perhaps by looking at some exceptions to that idea or maybe looking at some of the cultural variations and influences that might be around, perhaps messages that give men the message that 'boys don't cry' and that sort of thing. I'd be interested in your thoughts about that and whether you think it might be useful to take a moment or two to examine that issue?

While this example relates to the issue of male gender stereotypes, the same strategy could apply when challenging a co-worker's (or indeed a group member's or audience member's) prejudicial or discriminatory remark about any group.

WHAT TO DO WHEN A PARTICIPANT ASKS A TOO-PERSONAL QUESTION OF ONE OF THE FACILITATORS, INSULTS THEM OR CROSSES ANOTHER BOUNDARY, WHERE THE CO-WORKER IS VULNERABLE

As a co-leader of groups or training sessions, there may come times where we need to step in to protect or support our co-worker. Examples include when a participant asks a question that wrong-foots our colleague, or perhaps asks a question that is too personal, or makes a comment that triggers our co-worker into a fight/flight/freeze response. At such moments, we have to make a quick judgement call. In general, you want to be there for your co-worker, perhaps by intervening gently but assertively and offering a reflective statement or using a Socratic approach to explore what is behind the statement or question from the participant. Sometimes, however, you may make a judgement call not to intervene so quickly. It may be that the situation is not so serious, and/or that you feel your co-worker can handle it. This is a subtle judgement call to make, and you can always discuss it in the de-brief to see how your co-worker experienced your intervention or non-intervention.

Here's how an intervention to support your co-worker might sound:

You hear a participant make a sarcastic remark in the group about your co-worker being the 'student' and that you are the one in charge. You intervene by saying, 'Terence, that's an interesting comment, and if I could just note with the group that we hold to a very firm principle as colleagues, which is that when we co-lead groups we are equals, regardless of how long we have worked as facilitators. So if I might just reflect on the point you have made, I wonder if you have any thoughts about why you might feel the need to make a distinction such as that? I wonder how we can reassure you that whichever one of us is leading a session, we are still both involved and we both have equal responsibility for the session and the process. How does that sound to you?' (Listen to his response.) (Then, you turn to your colleague.) 'Judy, as we have discussed in previous groups, this does occasionally arise as an issue, and I'm glad that Terence has mentioned it so we can address it now. So thanks, Terence, and Judy can I hand back to you?'

WHAT TO DO WHEN IT APPEARS THAT A PARTICIPANT HAS A PATTERN OF TRYING TO PROVOKE, IMPRESS OR INTIMIDATE (OR IS OTHERWISE ACTING OUT AGAINST) A FACILITATOR OR GROUP MEMBER

There are times when the interactions between facilitators or trainers and the group can become tricky and even threatening. This will of course depend on the type of group you are facilitating or training. If a group member is becoming angry, or is behaving in an intimidating manner, or is behaving very distinctly in some other way that seems to be functioning to get a reaction of some kind from the facilitators, it is important at some point to raise the issue with the participant. Usually this should be done in the group, but in some cases you may decide to have the initial conversation one to one. When raising the issue, it is important for the facilitators to name what is occurring but also to maintain their credibility and strengths as group leaders. I saw the acclaimed drama-in-education pioneer Dorothy Heathcote model a particularly adept response when challenging a highly volatile young man who was provoking her during a session. It went something like this:

> *Dorothy to the young man and the group:* Let's all pause. Something interesting is happening. Paul, if I may say, sometimes I have the impression that you would like to get a reaction from me, or even that you are waiting for me to get angry with you and shout at you to calm down. Is there something you need to say or something we need to agree so that you feel it's OK to proceed? Is there something I am missing? I want to hear you.

In this situation, I recall Paul settling down immediately. He said what he wanted to say, looked a little self-conscious and then began to get involved with the larger group activity. What is particularly noticeable about this approach is that Dorothy referred to anger but in the abstract – as a possible reaction that she seemed to be invited to have – and this is very different from saying she was feeling angry. I have used this technique myself on many occasions, and it seems very effective at deflecting a heated exchange while also opening up discussion so that the person who is acting out gets a chance to air their views, but in a much calmer encounter. It's a great technique for avoiding head to head arguments with participants while also opening up discussion and debate.

WHAT CAN I DO IF MY CO-WORKER HAS PSYCHOLOGICALLY 'CHECKED OUT' OF THE SESSION, IS BEGINNING TO DRIFT OFF TO SLEEP, OR IS DAYDREAMING?

This is something that can happen to anyone on occasion. If this happens to you, and you see your co-worker drifting into a private reverie, there is a simple but gentle three-step method you can use to bring them back on board while also being pro-social and entirely good willed. First, you say their name; second, you reinforce their professionalism, skills and knowledge, and third, you let them know you'll come to them in a moment – this gives them time to gather their thoughts and orient themselves to what's going on in the session. Here's an example of how it might sound:

Lead worker sees that her co-worker, Stephen, has drifted off and is clearly not psychologically present in the room: Stephen (Stephen responds by looking at the lead worker), I know that (Y) is a topic that we have discussed in previous groups, and it's often a source of very fruitful debate. It's important to note that (participant) has opened up this topic and perhaps we'll look further at that now. Stephen, I'd like to draw you in to the conversation in just a moment as I know this is a topic where you have a lot of experience.

It is hoped that when such a method is used, Stephen is helped to reorient himself. His lead worker has also made it clear that she needs his input, but that she is also aware that he needs a little time to gather his thoughts.

Note: this technique can be used, with only a small adaptation, to bring in a group member who has drifted off.

WHAT TO DO IF A PARTICIPANT IS BEING VERBALLY AGGRESSIVE AND ABUSIVE TOWARDS YOUR CO-WORKER

In a situation where a member of the group is being heated and aggressive with your co-worker, you may make the judgement call to speak up and intervene immediately, as you see things are about to escalate to a highly volatile situation. In this instance, you can come in and use some de-escalation techniques. As an example:

Co-worker (sitting back down to leave only the man still standing – this way he is likely to sit): Adrian, I think we can all see that this is clearly an important point for you and you have some very strong views. Let's all just take a moment (you are indicating his seat, but not insisting; you want to give him options) and try to make sure we hear the point you are making, Adrian. Now if I'm right I heard you say (Z). Do I have that right? (He replies.) Thanks, Adrian, now I wonder if you could say more about that just so we are all clear, and then Joe [he is your co-worker] I think we can open it up to the group because this is an issue that affects everyone to one degree or another. What do you think?

Questions to consider:

- What is my understanding of why, with some co-workers, mindful co-working may be an unrealistic expectation, and may invite exploitation?

- What is my understanding of how co-working 'mistakes' or tricky situations can be re-framed as opportunities for pro-social modelling?

- In the past, what have I tended to do when faced with the sorts of tricky situations and 'what not to do's covered in this chapter?

- What are three potential difficulties we may face as co-workers? Let's make a plan about how to prevent them and also to deal with them when they do arise.

Afterword

The ideas in this book have been road tested during hundreds of staff development workshops over the past 15 years. It is a privilege to share these ideas with you, and I hope that you and your colleagues have found something useful here. If this book helps just one co-working pair or team to improve the way they communicate and carry out their work each day, it will have been worthwhile.

I had a very confirming experience during the final phase of writing this book that I would like to share with you. I was working in Melbourne for several weeks, and during the evenings and on the weekends I wrote portions of the book in the relaxed and friendly atmosphere of the Little Creatures Dining Hall on Brunswick Street. As I worked away, some of the staff became curious about what I was writing. When I explained it was a book about co-working, they all had something to say about how well they all co-work at their restaurant. I had to agree; it is surely one of the friendliest, most collaborative and smooth running restaurants one could ever hope to visit. As staff came on shift, they received hugs and warm greetings. Communication was smooth and seemingly effortless. Tasks and information would be passed back and forth in an elegant choreography, gentle touches and warm smiles smoothing the way. Nothing was a problem. Hundreds of customers were served at a time, and at peak moments, all the staff increased their pace but kept their ease. It's a remarkable place, and really rather perfect for finishing a book on mindful co-working. (Oh, and the food's great, too.)

During a quiet spell, I asked Britt, a member of the serving team, what she felt were the ingredients that made co-working so easy there.

She replied, 'I think it's respect first of all, and how well we communicate with each other. We all help each other, particularly when it gets busy. And we pass on skills to the newer staff, show them how things are done. It's pretty smooth.'

I told her that she had just about summed up the whole of the book in a few sentences, and we laughed together.

A few points I'd like to conclude with:

- If you are really smart, that's great and it's a good start. But that does not necessarily equate to great co-working. Being smart is in some ways the easy bit. Being cheerful, helpful, interested, generous, humble, and most of all, mindful – that's the hard bit.

- Always strive to make your co-workers look good. And praise them to others, especially superiors. This approach makes everything more buoyant and helps people progress. In a nutshell: *Be excellent to each other.*

- Make your life at work a daily delight, full of mindful, deliberate, self-aware communication and good humour. You have all the tools to do this. It starts with you.

- If you are a manager, you can have an even more powerful influence on organizational culture. One of the primary roles and responsibilities of senior colleagues is to encourage and develop the younger staff, and to be role models. One day, they'll run the place.

Finally, some practice knowledge from my great friend and co-trainer, the late Tony Morrison, who would often complete a training event by sharing this wisdom, taught to him by a community nurse. It goes like this:

> We all need three people in our support network. They might be three people or they could all be one person, but we need to have all three: we need someone to give us a shoulder to cry on, someone to scratch our head, and someone to give us a kick in the butt when we need to get a move on.

Good luck as you cultivate your own support network.

APPENDIX I

Features of Mindful Communication between Adults

In Chapter 1, when we considered the first principle of mindful co-working, we looked at the importance of adult-to-adult communication in the workplace. This appendix expands on the concept by exploring in detail what it means to communicate as a mature, integrated, mindful adult. The term *integration*, as I am using it here, means that we can bring together different aspects of ourselves into a working and well-functioning whole.

The features of mindful communication and integration that are outlined in this appendix are themselves integrated from a range of sources. The ideas are drawn from fields such as social psychology, positive psychology and psychotherapy. Most particularly, I have drawn from role theory[1] and dynamic-maturational attachment theory,[2][3] two developmental theories which underpin my approach to training and psychotherapy. Together these theories offer some very useful guidance about what it means to be a psychologically well-adjusted adult and also what it means to be able to relate to others in a balanced, integrated manner. This is crucial information,

---

1   Blatner, A. (2007) 'The Role of the Meta-Role: An Integrative Element in Psychology.' In C. Baim, J. Burmeister, and M. Maciel (eds) *Psychodrama: Advances in Theory and Practice.* London: Routledge.

2   Crittenden, P. and Landini, A. (2011) *Assessing Adult Attachment: A Dynamic-maturational Approach to Discourse Analysis.* New York: Norton.

3   Harms, P. (2011) 'Adult Attachment Styles in the Workplace.' *Management Department Faculty Publications.* Paper 81. Available at http://digitalcommons.unl.edu/managementfacpub/81, accessed on 30 September 2013.

because mature communication is at the heart of mindful co-working.

This appendix is intended to be used either as a general reference, or as a tool for self-assessment. As you read, you may wish to consider which areas you feel are strong points and which areas you can still develop. You can also use this appendix as a topic for discussion in supervision and in planning and de-brief sessions with your co-workers.

THE FIVE DOMAINS OF MINDFUL COMMUNICATION

I have divided the key features of mindful communication into five domains. These are categories of convenience and should not be applied rigidly. The domains are:

1. self-understanding
2. flexibility and adaptability
3. self-regulation
4. optimism
5. interpersonal communication.

You might notice that the first four of the five domains mainly focus on what is happening in the individual, and only the last of the domains focuses on interpersonal communication per se. This gives us a powerful indication of how mindful communication begins with mindful attention to our inner processes. We will now look at the domains and their functions in detail.

1. Self-understanding
Meta-cognition

This is the ability to think about our thinking and to capitalize on that thinking by having a new thought – that is, one that we have never thought before. Meta-cognition is also crucial because it is the function that helps us to spot discrepancies between our beliefs and our actions, or our memory of events and the stories we have previously told ourselves about those events. Meta-cognition is the process that allows us to self-monitor and see that we may be slipping into old patterns of response. We can also spot discrepancies in conclusions we have drawn about events in the past. This opens the door to new conclusions and new understandings of our life stories.

Reflective function

This is our ability to look inward and to get curious about what is happening in our thoughts, feelings and bodily sensations. Reflective function is also crucial in thinking about process issues such as transference, projection and other 'hidden' processes that can affect our relationships with colleagues. When we reflect on these processes, we treat this as useful information and use this insight to formulate new ideas and plans of action. Using our reflective function, we are also able to see changes in us over time, to detect patterns, and to envision how we might be in the future. Reflective function is one of the hallmarks of living fully and consciously.

Internal investigation

Mindful communicators are curious about themselves and how their mind works. They are interested in the process of personal change and appreciate that accurate self-understanding is a process that demands curiosity about ourselves and our patterns of response. They actively search for meaning in human interaction, and try to avoid jumping to conclusions about other people and their motivations. This function can also be thought of as 'inner interviewing'[4] – exploring the repertoire of roles and responses that occur in our inner landscape.

Integrating the past with the present

When we integrate the past with the present, it means that we have resolved events from the past. This means we have left in the past what belongs to the past, while also retaining the right amount of information from the past to help us function well and protect ourselves in the present. We are aware of what 'triggers' us and when we are being triggered. Mindful communication relies on colleagues being able to recognize when events and patterns of response from the past are being activated, so that these patterns of response can

---

4   Blatner, A. (2007) 'The Role of the Meta-Role: An Intergrative Element in Psychology.' In C. Baim, J. Burmeister and M. Maciel (eds) *Psychodrama: Advances in Theory and Practice*. London: Routledge, p.59.

be regulated. If we are going to be mindful communicators, we have to know when to let go gently of old patterns of response that are no longer useful.

Rational regarding predictability

Mindful and integrated adults are realistic about what they can and cannot predict. Their reasoning is based on the integration of information from the past and the present, with a realistic view of the long-term consequences of their actions.

2. Flexibility and adaptability

Allows complex causation

People who have flexible and resilient minds understand that many events in life don't have just a single cause. Rather, most events happen as a result of a complex chain of interconnected events.

Distributes responsibility accurately

This means that when we consider events we are able to identify who was involved in the event and who was differentially responsible for the event. We are able to make distinctions about levels of maturity, age, experience, power, authority and other factors which will allow us accurately to distribute responsibility for events. If we blamed ourselves as children for our parents' alcoholism, as adults we are able to see that it was not as simple as that. We can revise the story and give back responsibility where it belongs.

Varied strategies

Mindful communication relies on flexible minds with access to a range of strategies. If we are mindful, the strategies we use are varied in the sense that we can pick and choose the 'modes' of behaviour – or roles – that we carry out in the course of a day or week. At times we may be highly emotionally expressive, at other times we appear inhibited. In mindful communication, we will be aware that we have these varied strategies and that we can modulate them as appropriate to a given situation.

Empathy for all

This is the ability to hold in mind very different views from other people and still be able to empathize with them to some degree.

This includes people with whom we have opposing views, including those who may now or may in the past have been in the 'enemy' role. To empathize is not to approve, excuse or condone, but it does mean that we make the attempt to see a situation from the other person's point of view as a way of understanding as fully as possible where similarities and differences lie.

Integrated thoughts and feelings

Mindful communicators are able to balance their use of cognition and affect – that is, thoughts and feelings. They are able to process cognitive information – for example information about time, place, sequence, cause and effect, if/then contingencies, facts and information – and balance these thoughts with information gained from their felt sense of their emotions. So, for example, they will be able to trust their gut when thinking of a situation, and they will be able to balance their gut instinct with cognitive information. Mindful colleagues realize that emotions such as fear, frustration, anger, and sadness are the kinds of emotions that can be important sources of information about what is important to focus on. If something feels uncertain or alarming, they don't discard that information, they use it.

Holds both negative and positive feelings

Mindful colleagues are able to speak about and express positive as well as negative feelings, and are open to discussing any feelings. They can hold in mind both positive and negative feelings about other people and events.

Perspective taking

Mindful co-workers are able to take their own point of view and also the point of view of other people. They can balance different perspectives in order to arrive at the most adequate understanding of an issue.

Appropriate focus on relevant problems

In mindful communication, colleagues are able to focus on relevant topics and problems, even when the material under discussion or the work being undertaken cause difficult or painful feelings to arise.

Sees human complexity

In mature communication, people are not characterized as all good or all bad. Mature minds perceive human complexity and do not label people as perpetrators or victims. Integrated adults understand that within one human being there may be victim roles and abuser/ perpetrator roles – and they can co-exist in one person. They see human complexity and feel complex emotions.

Creativity and aesthetic sensibility

This is the ability to generate new and useful ideas and approaches – the ability to think outside of the box. Creativity is essential in a changing world, where novel solutions are needed. Related to this is our ability to cultivate an aesthetic sensibility, for example an appreciation of subtle distinction, philosophy, or any form of artistic expression, and to draw upon this sensibility in enhancing the co-working relationship. One example is when co-workers might decide, for example, to paint or draw together a co-created work of art that explores their co-working relationship. This form of communication can deepen a co-working relationship, as colleagues grow to understand each other in ways that reach beyond language.

3. Self-regulation
Evaluate, then speak

In mindful communication, colleagues self-regulate their thoughts and feelings in the sense that they evaluate a situation first, and then speak.

Mature emotions

Mindful adults are able to experience a broad range of emotions, and when speaking of events, the emotion and the content will have a sense of congruence. The words and the music go together, so to speak.

Stable values

Mindful individuals have a strong internal sense of self and of their values, which are stable over time. We know what is important to us at the deepest level. Our values do not shift with the wind, although they may evolve slowly as we move through various life stages, mature and learn from life experience. This might also be thought of as the part ourselves that is the internal philosopher, making meaning of our lives and our relationships with other people.

Self-leadership

Being able to lead ourselves means that we understand our values and we orient our energies in that direction. This is self-leadership. It means we can integrate and balance a very wide range of impulses and internal dynamics in directions that we consciously intend. It also means we make positive choices about how we self-regulate. This is good old fashioned willpower.

Can contain difficult and painful emotions

In mindful communication, colleagues are able to register that emotions are running high – both in themselves and others – and they are able to act as a container for these emotions. That is, they are able to tolerate even very powerful feelings, especially difficult and painful feelings, without acting them out against other people in insensitive ways, or allowing them to 'leak' into interactions with colleagues. Moreover, they do not allow these emotions to turn inwards and eat away at the self. Instead, strong emotion is recognized, given meaning, modulated as appropriate to the context and used to inform action. They are not afraid of anger, sadness or fear – they acknowledge their vulnerability and show an understanding of what other people experience.

Accepts negative effects of events

Integrated and mindful adults understand that sometimes bad things happen and these events can have negative and even devastating effects on us and other people. They do not dismiss these negative effects or minimize or deny these effects. Instead, pain, fear, loss, grief, crises of various kinds, anger – all of these emotions are allowed to be present where negative effects are experienced.

Accepts that some information is ambiguous/uncertain/incomplete

In mindful communication, colleagues realize that some information may remain unknown. This is acknowledged, not denied.

Able to arrive at difficult conclusions/ experience difficult or painful feelings

In mindful communication, colleagues are able to address difficult subjects and reach painful conclusions. They do not bury their heads in the sand and pretend it isn't happening, nor do they minimize the distress they are experiencing. This includes being able to experience grief, remorse, guilt and regret.

Self-compassion

If we are allowing ourselves to explore and experience these deep emotions, some of which may be painful and difficult, and we are also involved in exploring at greater depth some of the home truths that we may have avoided seeing in the past, it is important that we also practise the gentle art of self-compassion. This is where we give ourselves a break and acknowledge ourselves to be flawed human beings like everyone else. We put things in perspective, and do our best to learn lessons and not make the same mistake again.

4. Optimism

Able to find the good even in difficult or painful life experiences

Mindful and integrated colleagues will be able to draw life lessons from negative events as well as positive events. When bad things happen, including bad things in the workplace or in the co-working relationship, mindful colleagues recognize the seriousness of what has occurred, and at the same time look to the bigger picture. They can find ways of seeing unfortunate episodes as learning opportunities, and even as opportunities to enhance their working relationship and the work they are doing together. This is also called re-framing.

Self-efficacy

Mindful colleagues approach their work with a spirit of confidence and efficacy that they can influence their future. Where people have experienced adversity in the past, they have a sense that things can be different in the future, and they work with anticipation of better things to come.

Resilience when under stress

In mindful communication, co-workers are resilient within themselves and also in relationships with colleagues. They recognize when work is stressful and they have strategies to cope, including sharing the load, which often happens organically as the tightly knit work unit joins together to perform the work.

Able to find the good in others

Integrated, mindful adults are able to see human beings in their complexity and are able to find the good in other people, even when that person is on the other side of an important divide.

Spontaneity and energy

In mindful communication, we try to remain in the moment and to understand that, in many ways, the only thing we ever really 'have' is the present moment. Spontaneity is our ability to meet the demands of the moment by either coming up with an adequate response to a new situation or a fresh and fully present response to a familiar situation. This also requires energy. Combining energy with spontaneity means we can access our inner resources and activate ourselves in ways that go beyond robotic routines.

Gratitude

Mindful colleagues are grateful to each other and thank each other in many different ways. It can take many forms beyond saying 'thank you', although that's really important, too. This subtle and skilled role includes being able to receive thanks, to appreciate, to enjoy, to celebrate the achievements of colleagues, and to allow them to celebrate yours.

5. Interpersonal communication
Long-term relationships

This is the ability to sustain relationships over time. It means we learn to trust and evolve as colleagues, and feel comfortable with getting to know each other better. We also find ways to keep the relationship fresh, and take mutual responsibility for doing so. (Chapter 1 offers many ideas about the co-working relationship and how to keep it functioning well.)

Boundaries

Mindful colleagues scrupulously maintain physical, emotional, social, sexual and personal boundaries in relation to other people.

Clear communication

In order to communicate mindfully, colleagues try their best to speak so that they can be understood by the other person, while also using all of their active listening skills to ensure they understand each other. Mindful colleagues understand that their communication style may need to shift depending on the person they are working with. For example, all languages have different registers – formal and informal distinctions being one of the most common. In order for colleagues to work together, there must be a common meeting place where people are comfortable with the tenor and mode of communication. This does not mean everyone needs to communicate in the same way, with the same accent or in the same register. It simply means that people need to understand and agree the norms of communication in the workplace.

Communicating feelings

Mindful colleagues are able to communicate their feelings and express needs and wants.

Cooperative

Mindful co-workers are cooperative in their interactions with colleagues. Interactions are not jagged or one sided. They engage well in the give-and-take of dialogue and co-working. They are able to tolerate differences of opinion and also to argue for their own beliefs without denigrating the other person. They have a willingness to find common ground and common purpose as opposed to insisting on across-the-board agreement and like-mindedness.

Able to mentalize

This is the ability to use our imagination to interpret our own perspective and also the perspective of other people. This includes our ability to perceive and interpret our internal state and to imagine the internal state of other people. It also includes our ability to interpret intentions in ourselves and others – for example, their feelings, needs, wants, goals and reasons. Most importantly of all, being able to mentalize means that we can adjust our behaviour towards the other person so that we both achieve our aims and feel respected and heard.

Rating scale for mindful communication in the workplace

Using the following items in Table AI.1, you can rate yourself, your co-workers, various teams you belong to, your department or indeed your whole organization in terms of the level of maturity and integration in interpersonal communication. Just as with the rating scale in Chapter 1, this rating scale includes a time line aspect, looking at past, present and future functioning. You can use it to set goals for personal growth and development, and also for broader goals in your team or organization.

TABLE A1.1: SELF-RATING SCALE FOR MINDFUL COMMUNICATION IN THE WORKPLACE

Name . . . . Rate yourself, your co-working pair, your team, your group or your organization on a scale of one to ten, with one being lowest and ten being highest. Use the scale to assess strength of communication and also to formulate plans for development.	One year ago (1–10)	Now (1–10)	One year from now (goal) (1–10)
Self-reflection and self-understanding			
Meta-cognition			
Reflective function			
Internal investigation			
Integrating the past with the present			
Rational regarding predictability			
Flexibility and adaptability of mind			
Allows complex causation			
Distributes responsibility accurately			
Varied strategies			
Empathy for all			
Integrated thoughts and feelings			

Holds both negative and positive feelings			
Perspective taking			
Appropriate focus on relevant problems			
Sees human complexity			
Creativity and aesthetic sensibility			
Self-regulation			
Evaluate, then speak			
Mature emotions			
Stable values			
Self-leadership			
Can contain difficult and painful emotions			
Accepts negative effects of events			
Accepts that some information is ambiguous/uncertain/incomplete			
Able to arrive at difficult conclusions/experience difficult or painful feelings			
Self-compassion			
Optimism			
Able to find the good even in difficult or painful life experiences			
Self-efficacy			
Resilience when under stress			
Able to find the good in others			
Spontaneity and energy			
Gratitude			
Interpersonal communication			
Long-term relationships			
Boundaries			
Clear communication			
Communicating feelings			
Cooperative			
Able to mentalize			

SUGGESTIONS FOR USING THE SELF-RATING TABLE, AND QUESTIONS TO CONSIDER

- How do you rate your level of mindful communication?
- How does this affect your communication with colleagues?
- How do you want to use this reflection?
- How can you use this self-assessment as an opportunity for growth?
- If you became more mindful and integrated in your self-understanding and in your communication, what benefits can you see for yourself, your colleagues and your organization?

If you feel that you have enough rapport with colleagues, you could try independently rating each other and then comparing scores.

- How do the scores compare?
- Where do you agree or differ?
- What's behind the differences?
- What evidence are you drawing upon to make your evaluations?
- How can you explore these differences and come out stronger?
- Who could offer you objective feedback?

Scenarios for Discussion and Training

This appendix presents eight scenarios for you to discuss with your colleagues, or you can use the scenarios for in-service training events or just for your own consideration. Each scenario illustrates a different way in which the principles and skills of mindful co-working are needed. In most of the scenarios, there are distinct gaps in mindful co-working. Each scenario is followed by a series of questions for you to consider. And in all but one case, the scenarios are fictional (the penultimate case is an actual case).

As you read and discuss the case studies, please try to avoid seeing the people in the stories as 'goodies' and 'baddies'. It may be tempting to do this in some of the scenarios, but the real challenge is to see both sides and to understand why each person feels right and justified from their point of view. You may also want to give some consideration to the other characters in the scenario who are just out of the picture – operating in the wings, so to speak. Consider what role they play in the scenario. This will help you to understand the broader, systemic influences affecting the characters. The challenge then is to make a decision about how to deal with the situation.

The colleague who said he was fine!

In a residential home for young people in care, staff member Jonathan has had a terrible night and is about to go off shift as Heather arrives for the day shift. She reads the handover notes and sees that one of the boys living in the home – Calum – tried to kill himself last night by cutting his wrists. Calum, who is 13, had as a young child been very badly beaten by his father. Yesterday he had accidentally seen his father in the street, and when his father saw him he drunkenly shouted abuse at Calum, saying he wished Calum had never been born, how his mother was a (expletive) and that he was going to kill Calum. Calum ran back to the residential home for safety, but he went into an emotional tailspin after that and told a member of staff that he feels it is pointless to grow up because his father 'will always be there, tormenting me'. In deep despair, late at night he tried to kill himself.

On investigating a sudden noise from upstairs, Jonathan discovered Calum very near death and called an ambulance. He spent most of the night in the emergency department with Calum, and just returned an hour ago to write up the incident. Heather looks in Calum's room and sees that there is still blood in the bathroom where Calum had tried to take his life. Heather returns downstairs to see that Jonathan is rushing for the door, leaving for home. She asks him how he is, and he says very brightly, 'I'm fine! Really, it's OK!' Heather, who has known Jonathan for five years, speaks very firmly but kindly to him, and asks him to sit down in the office to discuss the events of the night. She says to him, 'Jonathan, I'm concerned about you. How are you feeling, really?' Within five minutes, Jonathan is in tears, explaining how afraid he was for Calum and how horrifying it was to find the boy in a pool of blood. Jonathan also speaks about his anger at Calum's father, and his fears for the boy as he grows older. Heather listens quietly and patiently as her colleague tells his painful story.

- What do you think of Heather's actions on that morning?

- What do you think was the function, or meaning, of Jonathan's response to her that he was fine? What feelings was he likely to have experienced during the night before? What is your understanding of how people cope with powerful feelings in such situations?

- Which of the five principles of mindful co-working (see Chapter 1) do you think are most relevant to this case example?

- Does anything like this ever happen in your workplace? How do colleagues respond to each other when emotions are running hot? Are people able to discuss and express difficult or painful feelings in your workplace, or are strong feelings off limits?

- What would you have done if you were in Heather's position, seeing Jonathan heading for the door?

The wounded colleague

During a team meeting in a corporate office, the team is going through a project management plan and they are giving Donald feedback about the number of tasks that he is behind on. Isaac and Gemma, who are jointly responsible for the completion of the project, are giving Donald clear and direct feedback. Donald is an able worker and he has a crucial role in relation to the task, but he has also been stretched thinly over several projects in different parts of the company. Mid-way through their feedback, Donald folds his arms over his chest and says that he feels like a schoolboy who is being told off by the teachers. He looks very upset and he offers to leave the project 'if that will make you feel better'. The meeting grinds to a halt and it becomes clear that the project is hanging in the balance, as there is no chance of completion on time and within budget without the input of all the staff involved – including Donald. The team leader attempts to soothe ruffled feathers but to no avail. Donald is much wounded and the two workers in charge of the project are fed up.

- What would you do if you were the team leader?
- What is the role of emotion in this scenario?
- What responsibilities do Isaac, Gemma and Donald have for the impasse?
- What happened to the adult-to-adult communication when Donald was under great pressure?
- What are the risks if repair is not made to this co-working team? How can the repair be made?
- How could the principles of mindful co-working apply in this situation?
- Which of the five principles of mindful co-working (see Chapter 1) do you think are most relevant to this case example?
- Does anything like this ever happen in your workplace? If so, what resources are available to help you and your colleagues take steps to prevent such episodes in the future?

The disheartened young social worker

In a busy urban social work department, Andrew, a first year social worker, has done an assessment of a struggling mother and her son who has turned 18, who has complex physical and intellectual disabilities. Andrew has agreed to try to help them access education, home support and physical therapy resources, which have all but stopped since the son turned 18 six months ago. The case is not the highest priority, because the mother up to this point has been coping well enough. Recently, however, her health has deteriorated, and she can no longer look after her son as she has in the past. A low priority case could soon become a crisis if help is not found for this woman and her son.

Andrew speaks to his supervisor, Margaret, who has just emerged from a tense meeting where senior managers were informing middle managers about a round of budget cuts to come soon. Margaret asks him, 'Is anyone dying!?' Andrew replies, 'No, no one is dying.' 'Then they'll have to join the back of the queue like anyone else! It's not a priority. You should not have told them you would look into it. You'll give them false hopes.'

Andrew is left feeling humiliated, patronized, powerless to help, and deeply resentful at the way the family was written off because it was not an emergency case, when he can see what is coming after the mother collapses. Andrew is so disheartened by the experience and the way he was spoken to by Margaret that he is thinking about leaving social work.

- If you were offering assistance to this social work team, what would you want to explore with Margaret and Andrew?

- What is the role of emotion in this scenario?

- What systemic issues may have influenced Margaret's sharp retort to Andrew? For example, what pressures were on Margaret that allowed her to let slip her professional role and respond in the way she did? Is she aware of how the interaction has affected the young social worker?

- What ideas do you have about how this situation can be repaired?

- How might the workers improve their mindful co-working?

- Which of the five principles of mindful co-working (see Chapter 1) do you think are most relevant to this case example?

- Does anything like this ever happen in your workplace? If so, what resources are available to help you and your colleagues take steps to prevent such episodes in the future?

The stressed doctor

In a large government-run community mental health service, a change in staffing has meant that a new staff member, Tamsin, is organizing the appointments for the doctors and nurses. Doctor Hamilton has had two patients arrive at the same time for a one hour appointment, and their appointment cards both read the same time and date. Patients typically have to wait several weeks for an appointment, so this is a serious blunder. One of the patients becomes irate and says she will be making a complaint because this has happened before and she feels she is wasting her time trying to get treatment. Doctor Hamilton storms into the reception area and, within the hearing of a range of staff and patients, she lambasts Tamsin, saying she is fed up with the inefficiencies and how the administrators 'keep getting it wrong'. Doctor Hamilton is not aware that the first patient's appointment had been made before Tamsin started in her post, and Tamsin had scheduled the second patient because some information was lost during the transition from one system to another. An honest mistake. Tamsin sits in stunned silence, and is later seen collecting her things, saying she may not be back tomorrow.

- What systemic factors influenced Dr Hamilton's unfortunate outburst in the workplace?

- What was the effect on Tamsin?

- What is the role of emotion in this scenario?

- How would you offer help and guidance to Doctor Hamilton? And to Tamsin?

- How do you think this situation could be repaired?

- How might the workers improve their mindful co-working?

- Which of the five principles of mindful co-working (see Chapter 1) do you think are most relevant to this case example?

- Does anything like this ever happen in your workplace? If so, what resources are available to help you and your colleagues take steps to prevent such episodes in the future?

The co-worker who wanted to go 'strictly by the book'

In a group work session in the community, run by criminal justice services, two co-workers, Brian and Denise, are leading a session. During the session, one of the group members, a man who is recovering from serious drug addiction, tells the story of his mother's death from an overdose when he was seven. One of the other men in the group says the same happened to him, and upon hearing this, the first man begins to sob. Brian shifts in his seat and makes a comment about that not being relevant to the man's offending behaviour. Brian says in a rather dismissive tone, 'Please don't tell us about your childhood – that's not what we're here to look at.' Denise, who is more experienced, gently prompts Brian to allow the group members to experience their feelings. After some moments, she helps the men to feel safe, and they talk about the pain of loss and how they tried to numb themselves and avoid feeling grief by taking drugs and running with a bad crowd. In the de-brief after the session, Denise asks Brian what he was thinking and feeling inside at the moment when the group participant began to weep. Brian avoids the question and instead says that he was just trying to stick to the scheduled plan for the evening and that the men were taking the session off course and having a 'pity party'. Denise feels silenced and does not know what to do.

- In your opinion, what are some of the issues underlying this process?

- What is the role of emotion in this scenario?

- What might Brian be struggling with? How did Denise manage to preserve the integrity of the session when Brian became insensitive to the men in the group?

- If you were offering some assistance to this co-working pair and their team, what issues would you want to explore with them? How, for example, can workers balance the needs of the programme manual with the feelings and memories that emerge for the participants during the session? What is the possible damage done when participants are shut down or rejected at moments when they become vulnerable in group?

- What would be the benefits that come when workers are able to hear, validate and offer a containing environment for such powerful feelings to be expressed? How can mindful co-working help this to happen?

- How is drug taking related to the experience of psychological pain? Why might it be relevant to explore issues of loss, grief and identity with the group participants, helping them connect those themes with issues around drug use and other criminal activity? How solid must the co-working partnership be in order for these deeper processes to emerge safely?

- How might Brian and Denise improve their mindful co-working? Which of the five principles of mindful co-working (see Chapter 1) do you think are most relevant to this case example?

- Does anything like this ever happen in your workplace? If so, what resources are available to help you and your colleagues take steps to prevent such episodes in the future?

The presentation that went wrong

Serena and Howard have equal seniority and status in a medium sized company that is branching into international markets. They each have more than 20 years of experience with their company in a range of roles. They are now both senior managers in the sales team. They have prepared a meticulous plan for a 30-minute presentation for potential customers in one of their new markets. It's a very important moment in their company's development and in their careers. During the presentation, Howard goes off script and delivers several of the slides that Serena had prepared. After she presents a shortened version of her segment, and with time running out, Howard restates four of the points Serena had just covered. After the presentation, several of the potential new customers are overheard saying that Howard and 'his assistant' had done a good job, but it felt like there was some competition between them. Serena is beside herself with anger, but Howard feels it went well. They are about to have their de-brief session.

- What would it be like to be a fly on the wall in Serena and Howard's de-brief session?
- What will each of them have to do in order to make the de-brief session a positive growth experience?
- What is the role of emotion in this scenario, during the planning, the presentation and the de-brief?
- How can Serena give Howard feedback without lambasting him?
- How can the repair be made such that the two of them can go on to do better and better presentations in the future?
- What might be the role of a third party to help them have this conversation, for example their supervisor?
- If you were there, offering help to Howard and Serena, what steps would you follow to help them process what took place, reflect on their inner and interpersonal processes, and make their co-working relationship stronger than ever?
- How could such eventualities be prevented in the future?

- What role did each of them have in the session going so off plan?

- Did Serena have a role in allowing Howard to do her segment and repeat her later points? What might she have done to regain her lead role after Howard did his segment early on? It might be important to explore how Serena adopted the furious victim role during and after the episode. This might be something to discuss with her. Likewise, Howard took the complementary role, which is that of the 'perpetrating man', riding roughshod over Serena's feelings.

- How could the principles of mindful co-working apply in this situation?

- Which of the five principles of mindful co-working (see Chapter 1) do you think are most relevant to this case example?

- Does anything like this ever happen in your workplace? If so, what resources are available to help you and your colleagues take steps to prevent such episodes in the future?

The staff group that descended into hell

In a hospital for vulnerable adults with learning disabilities and autism, a number of support workers have begun to take out their aggression on the residents. They shout at the residents and handle them roughly. Residents are regularly given humiliating punishments and are wrestled to the ground in 'play fights'. The care descends to cruel and sadistic levels of treatment. Crucially, some of the newer staff feel unable to challenge the status quo, and they feel unable to inform the management, who seem aloof and uninterested. The staff who have worked on the unit for several years, some of whom ostensibly have a managerial role, make cruel jokes about the residents.

This scenario is based on the notorious case of Winterbourne View Hospital in the UK in 2011. The case made national headlines and criminal charges were filed against some of the staff. A serious case review was written about the hospital.[1]

---

1   Flynn, M. (2012) *Winterbourne View Hospital: A Serious Case Review.* Gloucestershire: South Gloucestershire Council. Available at http://hosted.southglos.gov.uk/wv/report.pdf, accessed on 30 September 2013.

- Thinking about how such a scandalous and sadistic regime could develop, what are the co-working and systemic influences that might have contributed to such an appalling state of affairs?

- What is the role of emotion – for staff and patients – in the development and maintenance of the oppressive regime?

- Thinking about the five principles of mindful co-working, how might adherence to these principles have helped to prevent such a damaging system to emerge?

- In the actual case, an undercover reporter secretly recorded the daily incidents, and the hospital was quickly closed. What examples can you think of where a whistle-blower or an undercover reporter was needed in order to expose a closed system?

The worker allowed to slide

In a busy government office, Jo, who used to be a capable worker, has been seen by her co-workers to be seriously underperforming for more than two years. She comes in late to work, has long lunch breaks and leaves early. She is often late for meetings, and her co-workers have come to the point where they work around her, never giving her responsibilities because then they know their own work will not get done if they depend on her. Despite this, Jo is still part of the rota and she is still assigned tasks and projects. She always finds an excuse not to be part of planning sessions, and she always leaves before a proper de-brief can be done. None of her co-workers has felt able to challenge Jo, because she has in the past complained that people need to make allowances for her illnesses, which seem to change on a weekly basis. She has had several supervisors in the past two years, none of whom have challenged Jo for her very poor work record. Their answer has been to pass the buck by shifting Jo to different parts of the organization. On several occasions, workers have left their department rather than work with Jo, and they are furious that nothing is being done about her under-performance. One worker is heard saying that she is embarrassed to work for her department, given how they are so inept at managing Jo. An outside consultant is hired to assess the situation, and reports the situation to the head office, so serious is the lack of management in the local office.

- Why and how do you think this situation was allowed to deteriorate to the point it did?

- How could it have been prevented?

- While this is clearly a situation in which the line managers neglected their duties to monitor and manage Jo's performance properly, what was the role of the co-workers in allowing Jo to continue in her posts for two years?

- What is the role of emotion in this scenario? What stopped the co-workers and the supervisors from confronting Jo? What needs to be in place if workers and managers are expected to be able to challenge someone like Jo? In particular, what is the role of senior management in setting in place principles of accountability and responsibility at all ranks?

- If you were one of Jo's co-workers two years ago, when she began to underperform, what would you do to help prevent the situation from becoming worse? What information would you need, and what back-up would you need? If you were Jo's supervisor two years ago, how would you handle the situation?

- How could the principles of mindful co-working apply in this situation?

- Which of the five principles of mindful co-working (see Chapter 1) do you think are most relevant to this case example?

- Does anything like this ever happen in your workplace? If so, what resources are available to help you and your colleagues take steps to prevent such episodes in the future?

About the Author

Clark Baim, M Ed, BPA, UKCP, works internationally as a trainer, speaker, psychotherapist, group facilitator, supervisor and consultant. He is a registered psychotherapist (UK Council for Psychotherapy) and senior trainer with the British Psychodrama Association. He is Co-Director of Change Point Learning and Development, providing staff training and development programmes in the mental health, social work, criminal justice, voluntary, education and private sectors, and he is also Co-Director of the Birmingham Institute for Psychodrama, an accredited psychotherapy training school. Clark is the co-author and co-editor of several books and author of numerous chapters and articles on various aspects of supervision, group work methods, psychotherapy, attachment theory, applied theatre and offender treatment. In his role as a trainer, he has facilitated – individually and with co-trainers – more than 2000 workshops, training courses and conference presentations in 15 countries. He is a Fellow of the Berry Street Childhood Institute in Melbourne, Australia and a winner of the Scholar's Award from the American Society for Group Psychotherapy and Psychodrama. Early in his career, Clark specialized in the field of applied theatre and was the Founding Director of Geese Theatre UK, a company focusing on offender rehabilitation. He is now the chairman of their Board of Trustees. He has worked in more than 200 prisons and probation centres across North America, Europe and South Africa, and he continues to teach and conduct research in applied theatre, psychodrama, developmental attachment theory and offender rehabilitation. A native of Chicago and graduate of Williams College, Massachusetts, Clark now lives in the UK.

OTHER BOOKS BY CLARK BAIM

Attachment-based Practice with Adults: Understanding Strategies and Promoting Positive Change. Co-written with Tony Morrison. Brighton: Pavilion.

Psychodrama: Advances in Theory and Practice. Co-edited with Jorge Burmeister and Manuela Maciel. Hove: Routledge.

The Geese Theatre Handbook: Drama with Offenders and People at Risk. Co-edited with Sally Brookes and Alun Mountford. Winchester: Waterside Press.

Understanding Perpetrators, Protecting Children. Co-written with Lynda Deacon, Bryan Gocke and Dan Grant. London: Whiting and Birch.

CONTACT THE AUTHOR

If you have enjoyed this book and found it useful, you might want to contact Clark Baim and his colleagues at Change Point Learning and Development for some practical training. If you want to learn more about available courses, please contact Clark Baim via mailbox@changepointlearning.com or visit www.clarkbaim.com.

Index